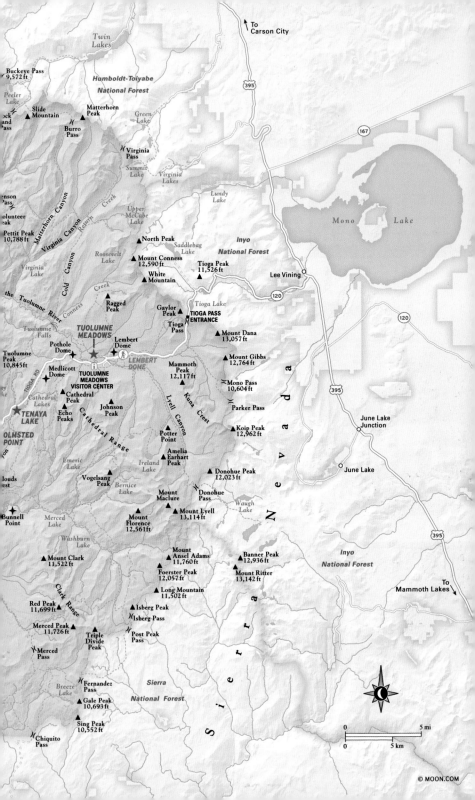

CONTENTS

58

102

140

187

194

208

Yosemite Valley as seen from Tunnel View vista point

WELCOME TO
YOSEMITE

Plunging waterfalls, stark granite, alpine lakes, pristine meadows, giant sequoia trees, and raging rivers—you'll find them all in Yosemite National Park. At 1,169 square miles (3,028 sq km), the park is nearly the size of Rhode Island. It's one of the most popular national parks in the United States, visited by about four million people each year.

Set aside as a national park in 1890, Yosemite is a place that is synonymous with scenery. The 7-mile-long (11.3-km) Yosemite Valley, with its 3,000-foot (900-m) granite walls and leaping waterfalls, is known the world over as an incomparable natural wonder. It is estimated that more than half of the park's visitors see only the Valley when they travel to Yosemite, even though it comprises less than 1 percent of the park.

Beyond the Valley lies the pristine high country of Tioga Pass and Tuolumne Meadows' subalpine expanse, bordered by precipitous mountain summits and granite domes. To the northwest lies Hetch Hetchy, a reservoir in a valley considered a twin of Yosemite Valley. To the south are Glacier Point, with its picture-postcard vistas, and the botanic marvels of the Mariposa Grove of Giant Sequoias—the largest living trees on earth.

sunset on Half Dome from Yosemite Valley

BEST DAY IN
YOSEMITE

Morning

1 Start your action-packed Yosemite day with a morning **Valley Floor Tour** around Yosemite Valley. You'll savor extraordinary views of sheer cliffs, plunging waterfalls, and polished granite without the hassles of driving and parking (page 55).

2 Next, make the difficult choice between the Valley's numerous waterfall hikes. If you have to choose one, the **Mist Trail to Vernal Fall** is the hike that every visitor should take. The 3-mile (4.8-km) round-trip hike ascends a granite staircase to the top of Vernal Fall. If you want more, keep going to the top of Nevada Fall for a 6.8-mile (10.9-km) round-trip hike (page 60).

Afternoon

3 After the hike, grab a quick lunch at the **Village Grill** (page 74).

4. Stop in at the **Valley Welcome Center** to watch a short documentary about Yosemite, browse the excellent bookstore, and learn from exhibits explaining the park's geology, flora, fauna, and human history (page 85).

5. Drive up Highway 41 to **Tunnel View** and survey the Valley from this sweeping western vantage point. El Capitan looms on the left, Bridalveil Fall cascades on the right, and Half Dome and its granite neighbors anchor center stage (page 51).

6 Proceed to 7,214-foot (2,199-m) **Glacier Point,** where you'll find one of the West's grandest viewpoints (yes, it's even better than Tunnel View). Snap some selfies by the rock railings framing the vista of Half Dome, Vernal and Nevada Falls, and the Merced River Canyon (page 101).

7 Backtrack on Glacier Point Road to the **Sentinel Dome and Taft Point** trailhead. Hike one or both of these spectacular short hikes. Taft Point grants you a more northern view that includes stunning El Capitan, and Sentinel Dome delivers the full wow factor, a head-swiveling 360 degrees of granite (page 102).

8 Head back down to Yosemite Valley, where you'll have time for a quick dip in the Merced River before dinner. **Sentinel Beach Picnic Area** is an easy spot to park your car and go for a swim (page 79).

Evening

9 Leave yourself enough time to get spiffed up for your reservation at **The Ahwahnee Dining Room,** where wrought-iron chandeliers dangle from a 37-foot-high (11-m) ceiling supported by massive timbers, and enormous picture windows look out over a grassy meadow (page 75).

10 After dinner, head over to the **Yosemite Conservation Heritage Center** to listen to presentations about wildflower identification, Yosemite's Indigenous people, the creation of America's national park system, and other educational topics (page 54).

 You're probably ready to hit the sack, but stay up a little later so you can walk around Yosemite Valley in the moonlight. In the spring months, you might even catch sight of the "moonbow" that glows around **Lower Yosemite Fall** on a few special nights each year (page 54).

ITINERARY DETAILS

- To see Yosemite Valley's famous **waterfalls** at their prime, plan your trip for **April, May, or June.** The falls are fed by snowmelt, the majority of which occurs in those three months.

- At any time of year, a visit to Yosemite requires careful planning. Yosemite Valley in particular is extremely popular and its handful of **lodgings get booked months in advance,** especially April-October. Book in-park lodgings and tours at www.travelyosemite.com. Park campgrounds also fill quickly; go to www.nps.gov/yose/planyourvisit/campgrounds.htm for information.

- The **Valley Floor Tour** starts operating at 10am daily. Reserve a spot on the first tour so you'll have time to fit in the rest of the day's activities. If you're an early riser and don't want to wait until 10am to get started, hike the Mist Trail to Vernal Fall first, then go for a tram tour.

- In most years, **Glacier Point Road** is closed due to snow November-May. If you're visiting during these months, stops 6 and 7 on this itinerary won't be accessible. A great alternative is to drive up to Crane Flat and take a one-mile (1.6-km) hike to the **Tuolumne Grove of Giant Sequoias.** Even if there's snow on the ground, you can snowshoe into this lovely grove of big trees.

- If you choose to visit Yosemite **November-April**—a great choice for solitude lovers—you are required to carry **tire chains** in your vehicle. In the event of a winter storm, tire chains may be required on roads within the park boundaries.

Curry Village tent cabins

SEASONS OF YOSEMITE

SPRING
(APR.-MAY)

Spring is a wonderful time for visiting **Yosemite Valley,** when its famous **waterfalls are at their peak flow.** First-time visitors would do well to time their initial Yosemite trip for April or May, when the Valley is at its most photogenic and the waterfalls are shimmering white-water cascades. Spring is a transition time in Yosemite. Temperatures swing widely from freezing at night to the 70s during the daytime.

Temperatures (Yosemite Valley)
Day: 70°F (21°C)
Night: 32°F (0°C)

Road and Trail Access

Glacier Point Road and Tioga Road are closed in the spring and winter months. The roads typically open sometime in June. A few of Yosemite Valley's trails, like the Four Mile Trail that climbs the south rim, may be snow-covered in its upper reaches as late as mid-May.

SUMMER
(HIGH SEASON, MAY-SEPT.)

Be prepared for **crowds** if you visit in the high season. Summer weekends are the busiest days and are best avoided, especially in Yosemite Valley. But summer and fall (June-Oct.) is when Yosemite's high country—**Glacier Point, Tuolumne Meadows,** and **Tioga Pass**—is open and accessible, so you have the most options for hiking and sightseeing.

In Yosemite Valley, summer daytime temperatures are typically in the high 80s or low 90s (30-34°C); nighttime temperatures drop to the 50s (10-15°C). Daytime temperatures in Tuolumne Meadows and Tioga Pass

summertime at Tenaya Lake

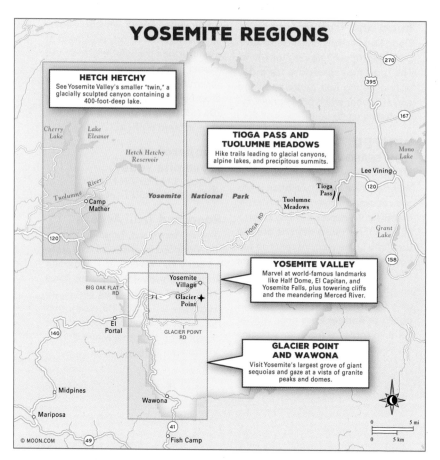

YOSEMITE REGIONS

HETCH HETCHY
See Yosemite Valley's smaller "twin," a glacially sculpted canyon containing a 400-foot-deep lake.

TIOGA PASS AND TUOLUMNE MEADOWS
Hike trails leading to glacial canyons, alpine lakes, and precipitous summits.

YOSEMITE VALLEY
Marvel at world-famous landmarks like Half Dome, El Capitan, and Yosemite Falls, plus towering cliffs and the meandering Merced River.

GLACIER POINT AND WAWONA
Visit Yosemite's largest grove of giant sequoias and gaze at a vista of granite peaks and domes.

Cherry Lake · Lake Eleanor · Hetch Hetchy Reservoir · Tuolumne River · Camp Mather · Yosemite National Park · Tuolumne Meadows · Tioga Pass · Lee Vining · Mono Lake · Grant Lake · Yosemite Village · Glacier Point · BIG OAK FLAT RD · El Portal · GLACIER POINT RD · Midpines · Wawona · Mariposa · Fish Camp

© MOON.COM

0   5 mi
0   5 km

in mid-summer are usually in the 70s (21-26°C); nighttime temperatures drop near freezing.

Temperatures (Yosemite Valley)
Day: 80 to 90°F (27 to 32°C)
Night: 50 to 60°F (10 to 15°C)

Road and Trail Access
In most years, all park roads and services are open by mid-June.

FALL
(SEPT.-OCT.)
Like spring, fall is a transition time in Yosemite, with temperatures swinging widely from freezing at night to the 70s (21-26°C) during the daytime.

Autumn is a fine time to visit Yosemite, even though most of the waterfalls will have run dry. The show of **fall colors** on the valley floor and the chance for **solitude** in this well-loved park are worthy reasons to visit. Popular sites such as the **Mariposa Grove** are easy to visit without crowds.

Temperatures (Yosemite Valley)
Day: 70°F (21°C)
Night: 32°F (0°C)

Road and Trail Access

Tioga Road usually closes on November 1 and doesn't reopen until June. The road may also close for a day or two during late September and early October when brief early-winter storms roll through.

WINTER
(LOW SEASON, NOV.-MAR.)

Winter is the **quietest season** in Yosemite. The lowest visitation levels are recorded November to March, except for the holidays. Many Yosemite fans think these months are the best time of the year. Visitors can see **Yosemite Valley** or **Wawona**'s giant sequoias crowned in snow, ice-skate on an outdoor rink with Half Dome as a backdrop, and ski and snowboard at **Badger Pass** near Glacier Point. In winter, always carry **chains** for your car tires, even if you have a four-wheel-drive vehicle. Chains can be required on any park road at any time, and that's federal law. And expect cold temperatures: At night, Yosemite Valley's air temperature will drop below freezing, typically in the 20s (–5°C), and daytime highs will peak around 50°F (10°C).

Temperatures (Yosemite Valley)

Day: 30 to 55°F (–1 to 13°C)
Night: 20 to 30°F (–6 to –1°C)

Road and Trail Access

Glacier Point Road, Tioga Road, and the Mariposa Grove Road may close as early as November 1. Wawona Road (Highway 41), El Portal Road (Highway 140), Big Oak Flat Road (Highway 120, from the west), and Hetch Hetchy Road are open all year except during extreme winter storms.

autumn colors in Yosemite

NEED TO KNOW

- **Entrance fee:** $35 per vehicle
- **Closest entrance to Yosemite Valley:** Arch Rock (Hwy. 140, western side of the park)
- **Main visitor center:** Valley Welcome Center (Yosemite Valley)
- **Hotel and park activity reservations:** www.travelyosemite.com
- **Campsite reservations:** www.recreation.gov
- **Gas in the park:** Crane Flat and Wawona only; none in Yosemite Valley
- **EV charging:** Yosemite Valley Lodge; the Village Store; The Ahwahnee; west of Tuolumne Meadows Store
- **High season:** May-Sept.

Yosemite picnic area in the snow

Lembert Dome

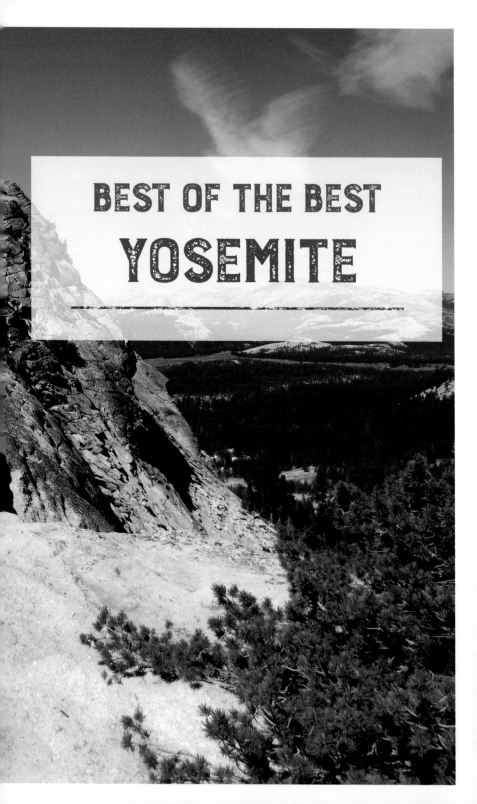

BEST OF THE BEST
YOSEMITE

BEST HIKES

UPPER YOSEMITE FALL
Yosemite Valley
STRENUOUS

Yosemite Falls holds the undisputed title of the **tallest waterfall** in North America. The upper, lower, and middle falls combined top out at a prodigious 2,425 feet (739 m). It's a strenuous 7.4-mile (11.9-km) round-trip hike to reach the top of the upper fall, but the base of the **lower fall** can be visited via an easy level stroll of a few hundred yards. Bring your rain gear between April and June; the fall's overspray drenches all who come near (page 56).

MIST TRAIL TO VERNAL AND NEVADA FALLS
Yosemite Valley
STRENUOUS

If you only have time for one hike from Yosemite Valley, this should be it. Of all the watery splendors that Yosemite Valley offers, a hike on the Mist Trail is the most exciting. The trail ascends a **granite stairway** to the brink of Vernal Fall before continuing on to Nevada Fall. The biggest thrill is hiking so close to the waterfalls that you get thoroughly soaked by their spray. It's easy to turn this into a loop by returning via the **John Muir Trail,** making for a 6.8-mile (10.9-km) round-trip hike. The Mist Trail is one of Yosemite Valley's most popular trails, but an early-morning start can help you beat the crowds (page 60).

SENTINEL DOME
Glacier Point and Wawona
EASY

Glacier Point offers one of Yosemite's most enticing vistas, and nearby Sentinel Dome, a 2.2-mile (3.5-km) round-trip hike, provides jazzy riffs on that same view. This bald **granite dome** rising to 8,122 feet (2,476 m) elevation offers a breathtaking perspective on Yosemite Falls, but that's only one small piece of its 360-degree panorama. Access is from the trailhead 1 mile (1.6 km) west of Glacier Point (page 107).

Upper Yosemite Fall (left); sunset at Sentinel Dome (right)

Mist Trail to Nevada Fall (left); climbing Half Dome's cables (right)

PANORAMA TRAIL
Glacier Point and Wawona
MODERATE TO STRENUOUS

The Panorama Trail traces a spectacular 8.5-mile (13.7-km) route from **Glacier Point to Yosemite Valley,** heading downhill most of the way and delivering nonstop views of a banquet of peaks, domes, and precipices. Take the morning tour bus from Yosemite Valley Lodge to the trailhead at Glacier Point, then lace up your boots. Follow Panorama Trail as it switchbacks downhill, providing ever-changing perspectives on Half Dome, Basket Dome, North Dome, and Liberty Cap. You'll also hike past **three major waterfalls**—Illilouette, Nevada, and Vernal—and miles of postcard-quality Sierra scenery. Finish out the trip at Happy Isles (page 110).

LEMBERT DOME
Tioga Road and Tuolumne Meadows
MODERATE

Glacially polished Lembert Dome is an example of a *roche moutonnée,* a dome with one gently sloping side and one side that drops off steeply. Rock climbers tackle Lembert Dome's south escarpment, but hikers can follow the 2.8-mile (4.5-km) round-trip trail around its east side, or the slightly shorter trail on its west side, then walk up the granite to the bald dome's 9,450-foot (2,880-m) summit. The reward is an **astonishing view** of Tuolumne Meadows and surrounding peaks, plus the chance to walk on Yosemite's surprisingly "grippy" granite (page 146).

HALF DOME
Yosemite Valley
VERY STRENUOUS

Reserve in advance to secure a **permit** for this epic hike. Start as early in the morning as you can because you have 16 miles (26 km) and a whopping 4,800 feet (1,465 m) of elevation gain ahead of you. Start at Happy Isles and proceed up the **Mist Trail** past **Vernal and Nevada Falls.** Above Nevada Fall, take the left fork for Half Dome. The trail is relatively easy from here (you've completed about half of the ascent already) until you reach the infamous **steel cables** that run up the back of the dome. It takes two hands and two feet to haul yourself up the cables, ascending 440 feet (134 m) of nearly vertical granite. On top, you can bask in your accomplishment while taking in the commanding view (page 63).

BEST VIEWS

GLACIER POINT
Glacier Point and Wawona

The commanding vista from Glacier Point, a 7,214-foot (2,199-m) granite precipice, takes in the park's most famous landmarks—Half Dome, Clouds Rest, Liberty Cap, Vernal and Nevada Falls, and the surrounding High Sierra (page 101).

TUNNEL VIEW
Yosemite Valley

Drive up to Tunnel View, just before the entrance to the Wawona Tunnel. Many consider this viewpoint, which takes in Bridalveil Fall, El Capitan, and Half Dome, one of the finest vistas in the park (page 51).

OLMSTED POINT
Tioga Road and Tuolumne Meadows

Olmsted Point provides jaw-dropping views of Clouds Rest, Tenaya Canyon, and a side view of Half Dome, plus high-country peaks and passes (page 137).

Tunnel View

BEST WATERFALLS

BRIDALVEIL FALL
Yosemite Valley

Bridalveil Fall in its 620 feet (189 m) of cascading glory is a must-see, and by the end of 2023, its short path, viewing platform, and restrooms will be completely upgraded (page 55).

YOSEMITE FALLS
Yosemite Valley

Lower Yosemite Fall is an easy walk, but waterfall lovers can't leave Yosemite without trekking to the top of its much taller sibling, **Upper Yosemite Fall.** Start hiking at the trailhead behind Camp 4, and after 3.7 miles (6 km) and 2,700 feet (825 m) of elevation gain, you're at a railed overlook that is perched at the brink of this behemoth. Yosemite Falls is the tallest waterfall in North America at 2,425 feet (739 m) (page 54).

VERNAL AND NEVADA FALLS
Yosemite Valley

Most visitors experience these two spectacular waterfalls by hiking uphill from Yosemite Valley's Happy Isles Trailhead on the popular **Mist Trail.** A 3-mile (4.8-km) round-trip will take you to the top of Vernal Fall; a 6.8-mile (10.9-km) round-trip gives you Nevada Falls as well.

For an all-day adventure, hike the **Panorama Trail** from Glacier Point down to Yosemite Valley. Just 2 miles (3.2 km) downhill from Glacier Point, you'll come to the lip of 370-foot (115-m) Illilouette Fall. Keep going and an hour or so later you'll reach the brink of Nevada Fall, then another hour

Bridalveil Fall

later, Vernal Fall. For this 8.5-mile (13.7-km) one-way trek, you'll need to catch the tour bus at Yosemite Valley Lodge in the morning to deliver you to the trail's start.

If you want to catch sight of Vernal and Nevada Falls without putting your boots on the trail, you can get a great wide-angle perspective from either **Washburn Point** or **Glacier Point** (page 60).

CHILNUALNA FALLS
Glacier Point and Wawona
Drive to the southern region of the park to see this lesser-known waterfall. From Wawona, hike the 8.2-mile (13.2-km) round-trip trail to Chilnualna Falls. The switch-backing path to this granite-lined cascade offers beautiful views of southern Yosemite, and the snowmelt-fed cascade is a perfect spot for lunch and a nap in the sun (page 112).

TUOLUMNE FALLS
Tioga Road and Tuolumne Meadows
For waterfall fans who are unlucky enough to miss the prime falling-water season in Yosemite Valley, there's still hope. July and August visitors can hike the Glen Aulin-Waterwheel Falls trail, a waterfall-laden hike along the Tuolumne River that leads past four falls: Tuolumne, California, LeConte, and Waterwheel. The trailhead is on Tioga Road near Lembert Dome and Soda Springs, and it's not usually accessible until July due to snow and wet conditions. This hike is a whopping 16 miles (26 km) round-trip, but with only 1,900 feet (580 m) of elevation gain—almost all on the return trip. The good news is that you don't have to hike the entire distance to enjoy some of the falls. The first, Tuolumne Falls, is only 4.5 miles (7.2 km) from the trailhead (page 153).

Nevada Fall

Vernal Fall

INDIGENOUS PEOPLES
OF YOSEMITE

HISTORY

Native Americans first came to live in Yosemite Valley about 4,000 years ago. Of the original tribes, the only one we know much about is the most recent, the **Ahwahneechee** people, who were part of the Southern Sierra Miwok tribe.

The last Ahwahneechee tribe to live in Yosemite, led by **Chief Tenaya,** moved into the Valley after the area had been vacant for some years. Stories are told of a fatal disease that swept through the Valley, probably around the beginning of the 1800s, killing most of its inhabitants and forcing the rest to abandon the area. These tales align with the fact that around that same time, Native American tribes throughout California were afflicted with the diseases that accompanied the Spanish missions.

Chief Tenaya, a Yosemite Miwok by descent, was raised in the Mono Lake area with the Paiute tribes. He had heard stories from his people about the glorious Valley, and when he reached adulthood, he traveled to see it. Finding it free of disease, he and about 200 others resettled the Valley. They called it Ahwahnee and themselves the Ahwahneechee.

The Ahwahneechee were skilled hunters who snared birds, netted and speared trout, and hunted deer, bear, and squirrels with bow and arrow. They gathered acorns from the black oaks and ground them into meal, dug plant bulbs in the spring, and set

Indigenous dwelling

the Valley's grasses on fire each fall to encourage better seed production the following year. They were also skilled craftspeople, making colorful baskets from willow, redbud, ferns, and strips of bark as well as practical tools like knives and scrapers from antlers and bones.

The End of the Ahwahneechee

When the cry for gold rang out across California in the mid-1800s, the Ahwahneechee tribe's future was suddenly and irrevocably altered. Gold seekers swarmed over the entire Sierra Nevada, and before long the miners and settlers demanded that the U.S. government place the estimated 10,000 Native Americans living in California on reservations. The state-sanctioned **Mariposa Battalion** was formed to round up the Indians.

After they were relocated to a Fresno reservation, Chief Tenaya and his people did not fare well. They were unaccustomed to the government food they were given and did not get along with other relocated tribes.

Tenaya's death signaled the end for the Ahwahneechee. The last remaining members of his band dispersed, some joining the Paiutes and others joining Miwok tribes along the Tuolumne River. A few Ahwahneechee descendants continued to live in Yosemite Valley over the next several decades, but their numbers were few.

NAMES

- **Hetch Hetchy:** The Miwok people named this valley "Hatchatchie" for a type of grass with edible seeds that grew here.

- **Tenaya Lake:** Named for Chief Tenaya, the last chief of the Ahwahneechee people. When told that the lake had been named for him, Chief Tenaya replied that the lake already had a name: Pywiack, or "lake of shining rocks." The name Pywiack now refers to a granite dome near Tenaya Lake.

- **Tuolumne:** The name of the river and famous subalpine meadow is the Miwok word for squirrel. Spend a few minutes in Tuolumne Meadows and you are sure to see numerous Belding ground squirrels, also known as "picket pins" for the way they stand upright on their hind legs.

- **Wawona:** Wawona was named in the Miwok tongue as "who-who'nau." "Wawona" represented hoot of an owl, the guardian spirit of the sequoias.

- **Yosemite:** "Yosemite" is a corruption of the Miwok word "uzumaiti," which meant grizzly bear. The Indigenous peoples that lived in the Valley were called Yosemites by European settlers and by other Indigenous tribes because they lived in a place where grizzly bears were common and they were reportedly skilled at killing the bears. The Mariposa Battalion named the Valley after the "Yosemite Indians" whom, ironically, they'd been sent there to evict. The Indigenous peoples of Yosemite didn't call themselves Yosemites; they called themselves Ahwahneechee, and they called the Valley "Ahwahnee" or "place of a gaping mouth."

SIGHTS

- The **Yosemite Museum** (Yosemite Village; 209/372-0200; 10am-4pm daily; free) is home to the Indian Cultural Exhibit, which interprets the life of the Miwok and Paiute peoples from 1850 to the present. On display are deerskin dresses and dance regalia as well as natural-fiber and beaded baskets. Rotating works of local artists are on display in the Museum Gallery (10am-4pm daily June-Sept., 10am-noon and 1pm-4pm daily Oct.-May), and the Yosemite Museum Store features local Native American arts and crafts.

- Behind the Yosemite Museum is the **Miwok Indian Village,** a year-round outdoor exhibit of local Native American culture. This exhibit is an excellent way to teach children about the Indigenous peoples who once lived in Yosemite Valley. Visitors can walk among traditional dwellings and watch live demonstrations of basket weaving and beadwork. A self-guided loop trail called "The Miwok in Yosemite" leads through the village. Interpretive brochures are available at the trailhead and in the museum.

- Native American tapestries and baskets can be found on display at **The Ahwahnee.** The hotel's gift shop also has a large selection of Native American art and jewelry.

ceremonial roundhouse

Tenaya Lake

BEST SCENIC DRIVE

TIOGA ROAD

DRIVING DISTANCE: 46.5 miles (75 km) one-way
DRIVING TIME: 1.5 hours one-way
SEASON: open June-September
START: Crane Flat
END: Tioga Pass entrance

Tioga Road is a scenic drive through red fir and lodgepole pine forest, past meadows, lakes, and granite domes and spires. Now a part of Highway 120, the road has an interesting history: It was built in 1882-1883 as a mining road to service the silver mines in the Tioga Pass area. It was realigned and modernized in 1961.

Along the way, be sure to pull over at **Olmsted Point** for a unique side view of Half Dome, plus stunning views of Clouds Rest and Tenaya Canyon. You'll also pass **Tenaya Lake,** with deep-blue waters and white sands that make it hard to resist pulling over for a picnic. Up next is **Pothole Dome;** even nonhikers will enjoy the short walk to the top of this low granite dome on the western edge of Tuolumne Meadows. Back in the car, you'll appreciate the grassy expanse of **Tuolumne Meadows,** the

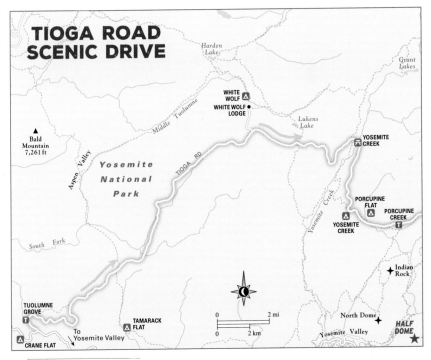

largest subalpine meadow in the Sierra Nevada. Another notable sight along the way is **Lembert Dome.** Take a 2.8-mile (4.5-km) round-trip hike around to the sloping back side of Lembert Dome and then climb to the top for a thrilling view of the high country. Or simply hang out at the base to watch the rock climbers strut their stuff.

Tioga Road

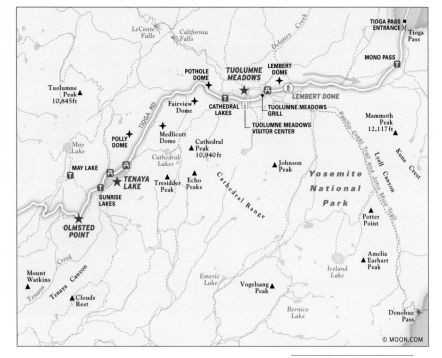

© MOON.COM

view along Tioga Road

PRACTICE SUSTAINABLE TRAVEL IN YOSEMITE

It's relatively easy to be a good Yosemite visitor: Properly dispose of all trash, stay on established trails, be careful not to pollute the water, and try to have as little impact on the environment as possible. But why not go a little farther in your efforts to keep Yosemite thriving? Make your vacation more eco-friendly by taking these steps:

- Don't purchase water in plastic bottles. Instead, bring your own refillable container and fill it at the free water stations located throughout the Valley.

- Ride Yosemite Valley's diesel-electric hybrid shuttles and all-electric tour buses. Yosemite was the first of the national parks to use zero-emission battery-electric buses.

- Rent a bike at Curry Village or Yosemite Valley Lodge, and tour the Valley without the hassles or emissions of driving and parking.

- Make use of the Recycling Center in the Valley, located behind the Village Store in Yosemite Village.

- Sometimes trash cans are hard to find, or they're already full. Carry a small bag to contain your trash, and pick up any trash you find that was left by others.

- Don't feed the wildlife. No matter how cute that chipmunk is and how much it begs, don't give it a crumb of your lunch.

Merced River in Yosemite Valley

YOSEMITE VALLEY

Seven miles (11.3 km) long and 1 mile (1.6 km) across at its widest point, Yosemite Valley is a mélange of landscapes. It is verdant meadows bisected by the clear Merced River. It is powerful waterfalls plunging thousands of feet over sheer granite walls. It is the forested home of a rich tapestry of wildlife, including black bears, mule deer, and chipmunks.

It is also the home of several hundred people who are employed in the park (or married to someone who is), and the destination of many thousands more who visit each day. It is a small city with sewage lines, garbage collection, a dentist's office, a jail, a courtroom, an auto garage, and a church.

The Valley is the centerpiece of Yosemite and the place where the vast majority of visitors spend most of their time. It offers the greatest number of organized activities of any region of the park, ranging from nature walks to evening theater, from ice-skating to photography seminars, from Indian basketmaking to rock climbing. The daily array of scheduled events and activities runs the gamut from highly athletic to nearly sedentary and can keep even the most ambitious visitor busy.

One of the best ways to travel around Yosemite Valley is by utilizing the free park shuttle buses. For route and stop information, see the Yosemite Valley newspaper that you received at the park entrance station.

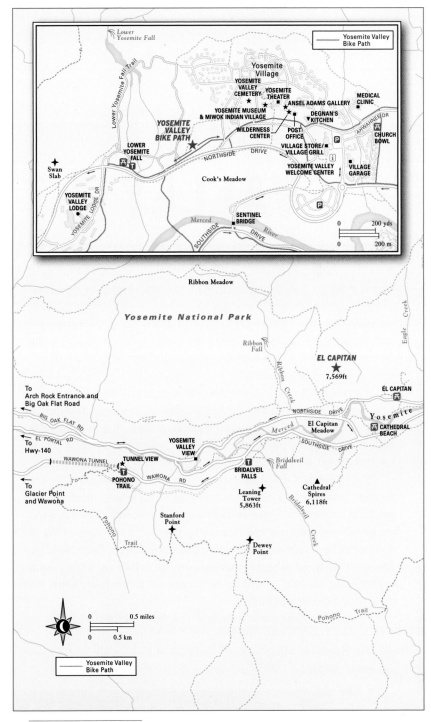

Yosemite Valley
Bike Path

Lower
Yosemite Fall

Yosemite
Village

YOSEMITE
VALLEY
CEMETERY

YOSEMITE
THEATER

ANSEL ADAMS GALLERY

MEDICAL
CLINIC

YOSEMITE MUSEUM
& MIWOK INDIAN VILLAGE

DEGNAN'S
KITCHEN

YOSEMITE
VALLEY
BIKE PATH

WILDERNESS
CENTER

POST
OFFICE

AHWAHNEE DR

LOWER
YOSEMITE
FALL

NORTHSIDE   DRIVE

VILLAGE STORE/
VILLAGE GRILL

CHURCH
BOWL

Swan
Slab

YOSEMITE VALLEY
WELCOME CENTER

VILLAGE
GARAGE

Cook's Meadow

YOSEMITE
VALLEY
LODGE

SENTINEL
BRIDGE

Merced

SOUTHSIDE   DRIVE

River

0   200 yds

0   200 m

Ribbon Meadow

Yosemite National Park

Eagle Creek

Ribbon
Fall

EL CAPITAN
★
7,569ft

EL CAPITAN

To
Arch Rock Entrance and
Big Oak Flat Road

BIG OAK FLAT RD

NORTHSIDE   DRIVE

Yosemite

To
Hwy-140

EL PORTAL RD

Merced

El Capitan
Meadow

CATHEDRAL
BEACH

WAWONA TUNNEL

YOSEMITE
VALLEY
VIEW

SOUTHSIDE   DRIVE

TUNNEL VIEW
★

POHONO
TRAIL

WAWONA   RD

BRIDALVEIL
FALLS

Bridalveil
Fall

To
Glacier Point
and Wawona

Leaning
Tower
5,863ft

Cathedral
Spires
6,118ft

Pohono   Trail

Stanford
Point

Bridalveil Creek

Dewey
Point

Pohono   Trail

0   0.5 miles

0   0.5 km

Yosemite Valley
Bike Path

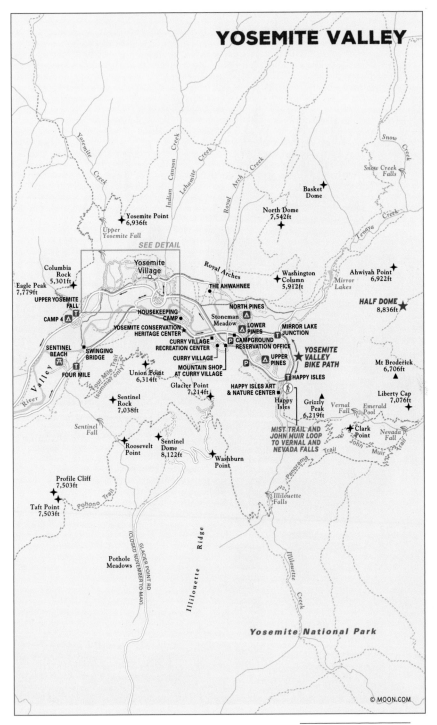

YOSEMITE VALLEY

Yosemite Creek

Indian Canyon Creek

Lehamite Creek

Royal Arch Creek

Snow Creek

Snow Creek Falls

Tenaya Creek

★ Basket Dome

North Dome 7,542ft

★ Yosemite Point 6,936ft

Upper Yosemite Fall

SEE DETAIL

Yosemite Village

Royal Arches

Washington Column 5,912ft

Mirror Lakes

Ahwiyah Point 6,922ft

Columbia Rock 5,301ft

THE AHWAHNEE

Eagle Peak 7,779ft

HALF DOME 8,836ft ★

UPPER YOSEMITE FALL

NORTH PINES

CAMP 4

HOUSEKEEPING CAMP

Stoneman Meadow

LOWER PINES

MIRROR LAKE JUNCTION

SENTINEL BEACH

YOSEMITE CONSERVATION HERITAGE CENTER

CAMPGROUND RESERVATION OFFICE

YOSEMITE VALLEY BIKE PATH

Mt Broderick 6,706ft

SWINGING BRIDGE

CURRY VILLAGE RECREATION CENTER

UPPER PINES

FOUR MILE

CURRY VILLAGE

Union Point 6,314ft

MOUNTAIN SHOP AT CURRY VILLAGE

HAPPY ISLES

Liberty Cap 7,076ft

River

Glacier Point 7,214ft

HAPPY ISLES ART & NATURE CENTER

Sentinel Rock 7,038ft

Happy Isles

Grizzly Peak 6,219ft

Vernal Fall

Emerald Pool

Sentinel Fall

Roosevelt Point

Sentinel Dome 8,122ft

Washburn Point

MIST TRAIL AND JOHN MUIR LOOP TO VERNAL AND NEVADA FALLS

Clark Point

Nevada Fall

Profile Cliff 7,503ft

Pohono Trail

Illilouette Falls

Taft Point 7,503ft

Pothole Meadows

GLACIER POINT RD (CLOSED NOVEMBER TO MAY)

Illilouette Ridge

Illilouette Creek

Yosemite National Park

© MOON.COM

TOP 3

⭐ **1. EL CAPITAN:** El Cap is the undisputed king of the granite monoliths and a mecca for daredevil rock climbers. Get a good look at "The Chief" from the meadow at its base (page 51).

⭐ **2. HALF DOME:** Your first look at this sheared-off granite dome always comes as a surprise, even though you've undoubtedly seen its image on postcards, calendars, and Ansel Adams prints. Hard-core hikers who secure a permit in advance can trek to its summit; everybody else can admire it from below (page 52).

⭐ **3. YOSEMITE VALLEY BIKE PATH:** Take a tour of the Valley along the Yosemite Valley Bike Path—without worrying about where to park (page 69).

2

YOSEMITE VALLEY 3 WAYS

HALF DAY

1 Start your day with an early-morning ride on Yosemite Valley's open-air tram. The two-hour **Valley Floor Tour** offers unobstructed, wind-in-your-hair views of iconic sights like Yosemite Falls, Half Dome, El Capitan, and Bridalveil Fall. A knowledgeable guide rides along and narrates the trip.

2 If you're lucky enough to be in Yosemite Valley when Yosemite Falls is flowing strong, be sure to walk the 1-mile (1.6-km) loop at the base of the **Lower Yosemite Fall.** Bring your rain gear in peak waterfall season (Mar.-June); the overspray drenches all who come near.

3 See the largest single piece of granite rock on earth and the climbers who tackle it. El Capitan, arguably the most famous rock-climbing site in the world, towers 3,593 feet (1,095 m) above the Valley floor. To watch the daredevils tackling this granite behemoth, wander out into **El Capitan Meadow** along Northside Drive. Binoculars are a big help.

4 It's time for another easy waterfall walk, this one to **Bridalveil Fall.** This 620-foot (189-m) cataract on the Valley's south rim drains a large watershed, giving it a dependable supply of water throughout the year.

5 Rent a bike at Curry Village or Yosemite Valley Lodge—or bring your own—and pedal around the **Yosemite Valley Bike Path,** surrounded by marvels everywhere you look. Twelve miles (19 km) of smooth paved bike trails let you meander alongside the Merced River, travel across the picturesque Swinging Bridge, and admire the majesty of the Valley's granite cliffs and spires.

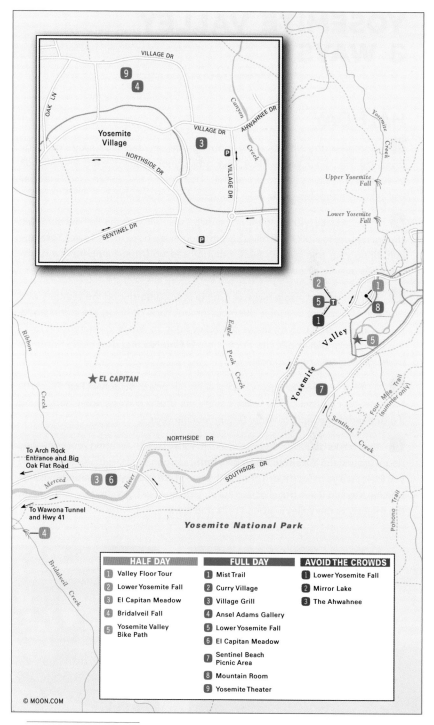

Yosemite Village

VILLAGE DR

OAK LN

VILLAGE DR

AHWAHNEE DR

Canyon Creek

VILLAGE DR

NORTHSIDE DR

SENTINEL DR

Upper Yosemite Fall

Lower Yosemite Fall

Yosemite Creek

EL CAPITAN

Ribbon Creek

Eagle Peak Creek

Yosemite Valley

Four Mile Trail (summer only)

Sentinel Creek

NORTHSIDE DR

To Arch Rock Entrance and Big Oak Flat Road

Merced River

SOUTHSIDE DR

To Wawona Tunnel and Hwy 41

Bridalveil Creek

Pohono Trail

Yosemite National Park

HALF DAY	FULL DAY	AVOID THE CROWDS
1 Valley Floor Tour	1 Mist Trail	1 Lower Yosemite Fall
2 Lower Yosemite Fall	2 Curry Village	2 Mirror Lake
3 El Capitan Meadow	3 Village Grill	3 The Ahwahnee
4 Bridalveil Fall	4 Ansel Adams Gallery	
5 Yosemite Valley Bike Path	5 Lower Yosemite Fall	
	6 El Capitan Meadow	
	7 Sentinel Beach Picnic Area	
	8 Mountain Room	
	9 Yosemite Theater	

© MOON.COM

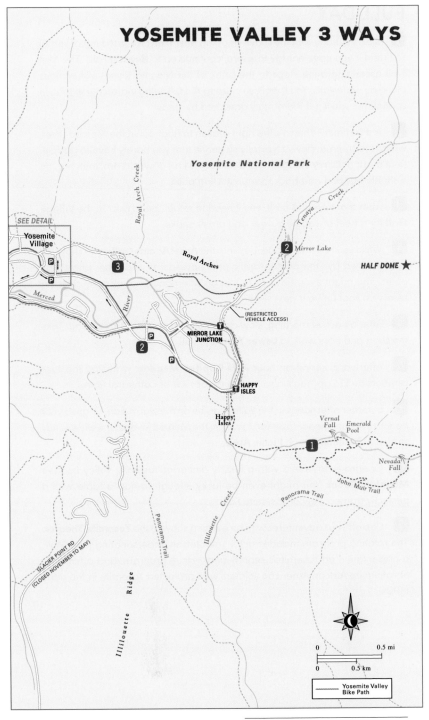

YOSEMITE VALLEY 3 WAYS

Yosemite National Park

Yosemite Village

SEE DETAIL

3

Royal Arch Creek

Royal Arches

Tenaya Creek

2 Mirror Lake

HALF DOME ★

Merced River

(RESTRICTED VEHICLE ACCESS)

2

MIRROR LAKE JUNCTION

HAPPY ISLES

Happy Isles

Vernal Fall

Emerald Pool

1

Nevada Fall

John Muir Trail

Panorama Trail

Illilouette Creek

GLACIER POINT RD (CLOSED NOVEMBER TO MAY)

Panorama Trail

Illilouette Ridge

| 0 | 0.5 mi |
| 0 | 0.5 km |

Yosemite Valley Bike Path

FULL DAY

1 Start your day with the show-stopping **Mist Trail** hike to the top of Vernal Fall (and if you have energy to spare, continue on to Nevada Fall). The Mist Trail ascends granite steps to the brink of the Merced River's voluminous plunging waterfalls. You'll walk so close to the billowing watercourse that, in springtime, you'll get thoroughly drenched by spray.

2 Is it summer? Then it's the right season to float down the Merced River, where the summer flow is typically so gentle that you barely have to paddle. Rent a raft at **Curry Village,** float 3 miles (4.8 km) downstream, then hop on a shuttle bus and ride back to your starting point.

3 After that hike and float, you'll need to refuel. Head over to the **Village Grill** for a beef or veggie burger and a milk shake.

4 While you're in the Village, pop into the **Ansel Adams Gallery** to shop—or just be awed by—the photographic prints by Adams and other photographers. You might even be able to join an afternoon photography class (or reserve a spot for your next visit).

5 After an active morning, slow down for some mellow sightseeing. Take the short and easy walk to **Lower Yosemite Fall.**

6 Afterward, spend an hour in **El Capitan Meadow** watching the rock climbers on El Cap. You'll also have a great view of Cathedral Rocks.

7 Summer afternoons in the Valley can be on the warm side, so grab your beach towel and head down for a swim in the Merced River at the wide sandy stretch at **Sentinel Beach Picnic Area.**

8 Celebrate day's end with a hearty dinner at Yosemite Valley Lodge's **Mountain Room.** You might even be lucky enough to nab a table with a perfectly framed view of Yosemite Falls.

9 Cap off your adventures with an evening show at the **Yosemite Theater.** The rotating program includes actor Lee Stetson impersonating John Muir, a presentation on Yosemite's search-and-rescue program, and a film celebrating the African American soldiers who protected Yosemite in the early 1900s.

AVOID THE CROWDS

The best way to avoid Yosemite Valley's crowds is to visit during the off-season, which is any time between October and March, except for holiday periods. In these cooler months, you won't want to swim in the Merced River or ride in an open-air tram, but you can choose from many other activities that aren't available in summer.

1 Winter visits (typically Dec.-Mar.) provide the chance to witness the "ice cone" on **Lower Yosemite Fall**—a sight that most visitors never get to see. All you have to do is get up early and get outside by 8:30am or so, before the sun rises high enough to melt it. Walk or drive to any spot, such as Cook's Meadow, where you can get a wide-angle view of the falls.

2 If snow has recently fallen, take a free, guided snowshoe walk with a ranger, or rent a pair of snowshoes at Curry Village and set off on your own. No matter how deep the snow, snowshoes will take you wherever you want to go, such as **Mirror Lake.**

3 Don't like seeing your own breath in the chilly air? There's no better time than fall or winter to cozy up in **The Ahwahnee** with a good book. Pick a comfy seat by a window in one of the hotel's public rooms, or opt for a couch near one of the mammoth fireplaces.

More Ways to Avoid the Crowds

- October and November bring an amazing autumn color show to Yosemite Valley. These lovely fall days are perfect for bike riding around the **Yosemite Valley Bike Path** to grassy meadows where the black oaks turn soft burnished gold, a subtle contrast to the cottonwoods' school bus yellow (page 69).

- Walk the path through **Stoneman Meadow** on the Valley's east end to see the leafy fall splendor (page 54).

HIGHLIGHTS

TUNNEL VIEW AND ARTIST POINT

The view of Yosemite Valley Tunnel View vista is a standout; you may recognize it from a famous Ansel Adams photograph. The wide-angle perspective frames the sheer face of El Capitan, the sparkling white plunge of Bridalveil Fall, and the hulking granite of Half Dome. If you want to take your own Adams-style photo, time your visit for sunset or early morning to take advantage of the best light.

If you want some exercise and are looking for an Ansel Adams-worthy shot without the Tunnel View crowds, hike up the steep **Inspiration Point Trail,** part of the longer Pohono Trail, which leads from the south side of the parking lot. At 0.5 mile (0.8 km), you'll come to an old road. Turn left and walk another 0.5 mile (0.8 km) to an obvious clearing. Here, at **Artist Point,** the view is nearly as wide as at Tunnel View, but you're 500 feet (150 m) higher.

From Yosemite Valley, take Highway 41/Wawona Road; the parking area for Tunnel View is just before the Wawona Tunnel entrance.

★ EL CAPITAN

The largest single piece of granite rock on earth, El Capitan (The Chief) towers 3,593 feet (1,095 m) above the Valley floor. It is arguably the most famous rock-climbing site in the world. Get a good look at this granite behemoth from **El Capitan Meadow.** Many park visitors sit for hours in this meadow, binoculars in hand, watching the daring climbers inch their way up El Cap's sheer face. Park at **El Capitan Picnic Area** on Northside Drive and walk to the meadow from there.

Another great way to get a glimpse of the climbers on El Cap is to hike to **Taft Point** (off Glacier Point Rd.; page 109) just before sunset. Because it's located directly across from El Capitan, as the light in the Valley starts to fade, you can easily spot climbers turning on their headlamps to prepare for a night spent on the rock.

El Capitan Meadow (left); El Capitan Picnic Area (right)

If it's just the monolithic rock you want to see rather than the climbers, a great viewing spot is **Cathedral Beach Picnic Area,** just east of the intersection of El Capitan Crossover and Southside Drive. Located at a kink in the Merced River that's away from the Valley's busy roads, this is a great spot for a picnic or a float while admiring the hulking profile of El Cap.

★ HALF DOME

Probably the most famous icon of Yosemite is the sheared-off granite dome known as Half Dome. Several spots on the Valley floor offer great views of this odd-looking rock formation. One is at **Mirror Lake,** or on the trail just beyond it, where you can stand at the base of the famous stone monolith. Other good viewing spots are at **Stoneman Meadow** (across the road from Curry Village), **Sentinel Bridge** (you can often catch a glimpse of Half Dome reflected in the Merced River here), or at **Tunnel View,** just above the Valley on Highway 41 (page 51). The undisputed best "drive-to" views of Half Dome are from **Washburn Point** (page 102) and **Glacier Point** (page 101) on Glacier Point Road. If you want to hike to the top of Half Dome, you will need to reserve a permit far in advance.

YOSEMITE VILLAGE

Yosemite Village is home to the Valley Welcome Center and a number of other sights and services.

Yosemite Museum
209/372-0200; 9am-4pm daily; free

The Yosemite Museum showcases exhibits on the life of the Miwok and

Half Dome

Paiute peoples. Behind the museum is the **Miwok Indian Village,** a year-round outdoor exhibit of local Native American culture.

Yosemite Valley Cemetery
across the street from the Yosemite Museum

The Yosemite Valley Cemetery is the final resting place of many notable people from the Valley's history. Among the gravestones you'll find the names of Galen Clark, Yosemite's first guardian; George Anderson, the man who first climbed Half Dome; and three members of the Hutchings family, including Florence Hutchings, the first nonindigenous child born in Yosemite. Purchase a guide to the cemetery at the Valley Welcome Center.

Yosemite Theater
www.yosemite.org; 7pm nightly May-Oct., less often in winter; $10 adults, free under age 13

Various programs are scheduled at the Yosemite Theater, including the award-winning film *The Spirit of Yosemite*. The film is shown daily on the hour and half-hour 9:30am-4pm.

Check the park newspaper for current listings of evening presentations, including shows on Yosemite's search-and-rescue program and *Yosemite Through the Eyes of a Buffalo Soldier,* which details the history of African American soldiers who protected Yosemite in the early 1900s. Tickets are available at any tour desk in Yosemite, or you can buy them outside the theater before the show if seats are still available.

Ansel Adams Gallery
209/372-4413; www.anseladams.com or www.travelyosemite.com; 9am-5pm daily; $65-95 per person, maximum 6 people

The Ansel Adams holds an astounding array of photographic prints by Adams and other famous photographers. The gallery also sponsors three- to four-hour photography classes six days a week. "In the Footsteps of Ansel Adams" is a guided tour with an experienced photographer-teacher. Students carry their cameras with them and learn how to take Yosemite landscape and nature photos. "Ansel Adams' Legacy and Your Digital Camera" is an instructional class focused on

Yosemite Museum (top); Yosemite Theater (bottom)

proper exposure, depth of field, shutter speed, and more. Other classes include "Ansel Adams' Legacy and Your Digital Camera" and "In the Field: Creative Smartphone Photography." Multiday workshops and private photography tours are also available. Make reservations in person at the gallery or by phone.

STONEMAN MEADOW
across from Curry Village, shuttle stop 14 or 19
This meadow, near Stoneman Bridge, offers some of the best views of Half Dome, especially at sunset.

YOSEMITE CONSERVATION HERITAGE CENTER
shuttle stop 12; 209/372-4542; 10am-4pm Wed.-Sun. May-Sept.
Built by the Sierra Club in 1904, this beautiful Tudor-revival-style building (previously known as **LeConte Memorial Lodge**) served as the Valley's first public visitor center and is now a National Historic Landmark. The structure's granite masonry and steep-pitched roof were designed to replicate the color, texture, and vertical nature of Yosemite Valley's walls. In 1919, the lodge was moved from its original location in Yosemite's Camp Curry to its present site east of the Yosemite Chapel on Southside Drive. Managed by a Sierra Club curator and more than 100 volunteers, the space hosts free **summer evening programs** (8pm Fri.-Sat.; free) presented by historians, writers, and photographers. Originally named for Joseph LeConte, a geologist and Sierra explorer, the structure was renamed the Yosemite Conservation Heritage Center in 2017.

YOSEMITE FALLS
Comprising lower, middle, and upper sections, Yosemite Falls is 2,425 feet (739 m) tall, making it the tallest waterfall in North America and the fifth tallest in the world. The only way to see all three levels simultaneously is to get up high on the Valley's south side, such as by hiking the **Panorama Trail** (page 110). Many points along the **Yosemite Valley Bike Path** offer fine views of the upper and lower falls; one of the best vistas is from **Cook's Meadow.** In winter, early morning visitors (arriving by 8:30am or so) have a chance to see the **"ice cone"** on Yosemite Falls, when an upside-down cone forms around the falls' spray.

Lower Yosemite Fall
Northside Drive, shuttle stop 6
No visit to Yosemite Valley would be complete without a walk to the base of Lower Yosemite Fall, the bottom section of the highest waterfall in North America. The lower section of Yosemite Falls is 320 feet (98 m) high. It's an easy stroll of only 0.25 mile (0.4 km) to one of the most thrilling sights in Yosemite, but you might as well walk the entire 1-mile (1.6-km) loop. The trail starts right across the park road from Yosemite Valley Lodge.

COOK'S MEADOW
across from Lower Yosemite Fall, shuttle stop 5
Surrounded by a boardwalk, Cook's Meadow is a less-crowded spot for viewing some of Yosemite Valley's granite icons, such as Half Dome and Sentinel Rock, as well as Yosemite Falls. Access Cook's Meadow by walking from the parking lot near Sentinel Bridge or the Lower Yosemite Fall parking area.

BRIDALVEIL FALL

This 620-foot (189-m) waterfall is easily reached by a 0.25-mile (0.4-km) walk from the well-signed parking lot just east of the Highway 41 turnoff from the Valley. The stunning view of Bridalveil Fall from the west end of the parking area will inspire you to take the short paved walk to an overlook near the fall's base. When the snow melts in springtime, Bridalveil billows with ferocious energy, and you can hear chunks of ice plunging off the lip with a furious crack. In spring and early summer, you will feel the sprinkles of Bridalveil's billowing spray.

The Bridalveil overlook also offers views of other falls nearby: Turn directly around, and you'll see **Ribbon Fall** flowing off the north rim of Yosemite Valley. At 1,612 feet (491 m), Ribbon Fall is the highest single drop in the park, but it only flows during the peak snowmelt months of spring. Also look for a waterfall on the south canyon wall, roughly across from Yosemite Falls, just west of Sentinel Rock.

VALLEY FLOOR TOUR

Yosemite Valley Lodge; 2 hours, departures hourly 10am-3pm daily summer, 10am and 2pm daily fall-spring; $40 adults, $28 ages 2-12, free under age 2

The 26-mile (42-km) Valley Floor Tour offers an interpretive tour through the Valley with easy viewing of famous sights like Yosemite Falls, Half Dome, El Capitan, and Bridalveil Fall. From late spring to early fall, tour participants are comfortably seated in an open-air tram; in winter, the tour takes place in an enclosed bus. Most Valley Floor Tours include a drive up to Tunnel View, just before the entrance to the Wawona Tunnel, which many consider one of the finest vistas in the park. Along the way, the tour guide remarks on the park's unique geology and history. Evening tours are offered on selected dates during summer.

Bridalveil Fall

BEST HIKES

LOWER YOSEMITE FALL

DISTANCE: 1 mile (1.6 km) round-trip
DURATION: 30 minutes
ELEVATION GAIN: 50 feet (15 m)
EFFORT: Easy
SHUTTLE STOP: 6
TRAILHEAD: Lower Yosemite Fall or Yosemite Valley Lodge
DIRECTIONS: From Yosemite Village, drive west on Northside Drive for 0.75 mile (1.2 km) to Yosemite Valley Lodge. Unless you are staying at the lodge, parking is difficult in this area, so riding the shuttle bus is recommended. The shuttle bus will drop you off at the official Lower Yosemite Fall Trailhead along Northside Drive. If you must drive your car, there is limited parking on both sides of the road, east of Yosemite Valley Lodge on Northside Drive.

It's so short you can hardly call it a hike, and the route is perpetually crawling with people. Still, the trail to Lower Yosemite Fall is an absolute must for visitors to Yosemite Valley. When the falls are roaring with snowmelt in the spring and early summer, they never fail to please even the most seasoned hikers.

About 10 minutes of walking from the Yosemite Fall trailhead brings you to the **footbridge** below the falls, where in the spring you can get soaking wet from the incredible mist and spray. By late summer, on the other hand, the fall often dries up completely. Be sure to walk the entire loop instead of just heading out and back to the fall; there is much to see along the way. And most important of all: If you really want to view the waterfall at its most magnificent stage, plan your trip for some time between **April and June,** during peak snowmelt. Seasoned waterfall lovers should also plan to visit on full-moon nights in April and May, when if conditions are just right, they are treated to the appearance of a "moonbow" surrounding the lower fall.

UPPER YOSEMITE FALL

DISTANCE: 7.4 miles (11.9 km) round-trip
DURATION: 4-5 hours
ELEVATION GAIN: 2,700 feet (825 m)
EFFORT: Strenuous
SHUTTLE STOP: 7
TRAILHEAD: Camp 4
DIRECTIONS: From Yosemite Village, drive west on Northside Drive 0.75 mile (1.2 km) to the Yosemite Valley Lodge parking lot on the left. Park on the far west side of the lot and walk across the road to Camp 4 (do not park in spaces marked Permit Parking Only). The Upper Yosemite Fall Trailhead is between the parking lot for Camp 4 and the camp itself.

At 2,425 feet (739 m), Yosemite Falls is the highest waterfall in North

footbridge at the top of Yosemite Falls

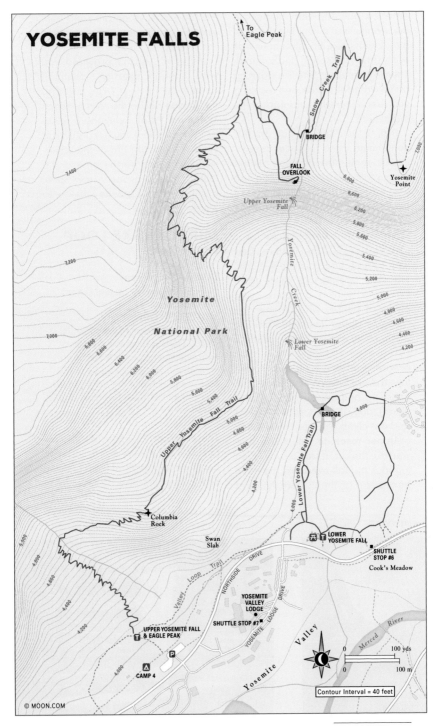

YOSEMITE FALLS

To Eagle Peak

Snow Creek Trail

BRIDGE

FALL OVERLOOK

Yosemite Point

Upper Yosemite Fall

7,400

7,000

6,800

6,600

6,200

5,800

5,600

5,400

5,200

5,000

4,800

4,600

4,400

4,200

7,200

Yosemite

Creek

Yosemite

National Park

7,000

6,800

6,600

6,400

6,200

6,000

5,800

5,600

5,400

5,000

4,800

4,600

4,400

4,200

Lower Yosemite Fall

BRIDGE

4,000

Upper Yosemite Fall Trail

Lower Yosemite Fall Trail

5,000

Columbia Rock

Swan Slab

LOWER YOSEMITE FALL

SHUTTLE STOP #6

Cook's Meadow

Valley Loop Trail

NORTHSIDE DRIVE

YOSEMITE VALLEY LODGE

SHUTTLE STOP #7

YOSEMITE LODGE DRIVE

UPPER YOSEMITE FALL & EAGLE PEAK

CAMP 4

Merced River

Yosemite

Valley

0   100 yds

0   100 m

Contour Interval = 40 feet

© MOON.COM

America and the fifth highest in the world. That's why hundreds of park visitors hike this strenuous trail every day in the spring and summer. There's no feeling quite like standing at the waterfall's brink and realizing you've conquered a landmark of this magnitude.

Still, if you tucker out on this demanding climb to Upper Yosemite Fall, remember that you always have a fallback option: You can hike only 1.2 miles (1.9 km) one-way to the **Columbia Point viewpoint** (also called Columbia Rock), ascending more than **100 switchbacks** for a total gain of 1,200 feet (365 m), and then turn around and call it a day. The view of Yosemite Valley from Columbia Point is a stunner, and plenty of people who planned on hiking to Upper Yosemite Fall turn around here and still leave satisfied.

Those who push on are also rewarded. After a level section and then a short descent, the trail switchbacks up and up until at 3.7 miles (6 km), and after a total 2,700-foot (823-m) climb, you reach the brink of **Upper Yosemite Fall.** Make sure you take the cutoff trail on your right to reach the **fall overlook;** the main trail doesn't go there. From the lip of

the fall you have an amazing perspective on the waterfall's plunge to the Valley floor far below.

If this trip hasn't provided you with enough exertion, continue another 0.75 mile (1.2 km), crossing the **bridge** above the falls to reach **Yosemite Point** (elevation 6,936 ft/2,114 m), where you get a stunning view of the south rim of the Valley, Half Dome, and North Dome, and a look at the top of Lost Arrow Spire, a single shaft of granite jutting into the sky.

MIRROR LAKE LOOP

DISTANCE: 4.6 miles (7.4 km) round-trip
DURATION: 2 hours
ELEVATION GAIN: 80 feet (24 m)
EFFORT: Easy
SHUTTLE STOP: 17
TRAILHEAD: Mirror Lake Junction
DIRECTIONS: From the Arch Rock entrance station on Highway 140, drive 11.6 miles (18.7 km) east to the day-use parking lot at Curry Village. Board the free Yosemite Valley shuttle bus to Mirror Lake Junction.

Thousands of Yosemite visitors walk to Mirror Lake every day in summer, but the vast majority of them miss the best part of this hike. The first thing

Mirror Lake (left); stairs on the Mist Trail (right)

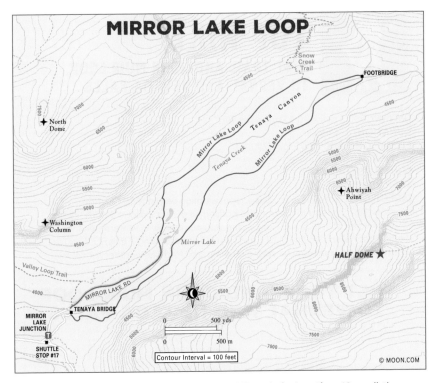

MIRROR LAKE LOOP

you need to know: Mirror Lake is not really a lake; it's a large shallow pool in Tenaya Creek. The pool is undergoing the process of sedimentation (filling with sand and gravel from the creek), so every year it shrinks a little more. Many visitors walk up and down this canyon, shake their heads, and ask each other, "Where's Mirror Lake?" If you know what you are looking for, the shallow pool is interesting to see, especially when its still waters produce a lovely reflective image of the granite domes above. But if you leave Mirror Lake behind and head back a mile (1.6 km) or more into Tenaya Canyon, you will get the most out of this hike, and perhaps find the kind of quiet nature experience that most visitors seek in Yosemite.

Start by riding the free shuttle from the Curry Village parking lot to **Mirror Lake Junction.** (Or walk there, if you wish, adding 1.5 mi/2.4 km round-trip to your hike.) From the bus stop, walk 0.5 mile (0.8 km) on pavement to **Mirror Lake** and check out the interpretive signs at its edges. Then follow the **foot trail** up Tenaya Creek for 1.5 miles (2.4 km), passing the left turnoff for the **Snow Creek Trail.** When you reach a **footbridge** across Tenaya Creek, cross it and loop back on the other side. Views of Half Dome, Mount Watkins, and their neighboring granite walls are spectacular, and the forested creek canyon presents an intimate amphitheater in which to view them. Find a boulder somewhere, have a seat, and take in the show. This loop trail is nearly level the whole way, and once you go beyond Mirror Lake and into the lower Tenaya Creek Canyon, you are likely to find a little solitude.

TOP HIKE

MIST TRAIL AND JOHN MUIR LOOP TO VERNAL AND NEVADA FALLS

DISTANCE: 6.8 miles (10.9 km) round-trip
DURATION: 3-4 hours
ELEVATION GAIN: 2,600 feet (790 m)
EFFORT: Strenuous
SHUTTLE STOP: 16
TRAILHEAD: Happy Isles
DIRECTIONS: From the Arch Rock entrance station on Highway 140, drive 11.6 miles (18.7 km) east to the day-use parking lot at Curry Village. Board the free Yosemite Valley shuttle bus to Happy Isles, stop number 16. In winter when the shuttle does not run, you must hike from Curry Village, adding 2 miles (3.2 km) to your round-trip. Trails may be closed in winter; call to check weather conditions.

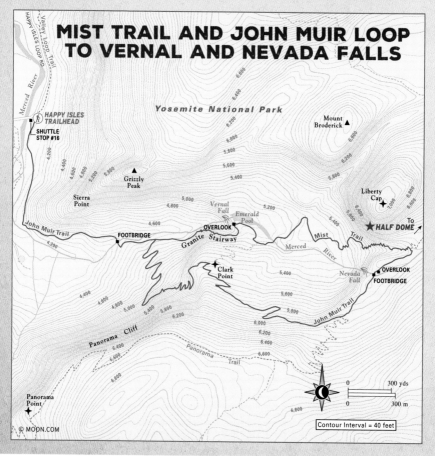

This is a hike that every visitor to the Valley should take, even if it's the only trail they walk all year. Despite how crowded the trail inevitably is, this is a world-class hike to one of the most photographed waterfalls in the world. Make your trip more enjoyable by starting as early in the morning as possible, before the hordes are out in full force.

Start by taking the free Yosemite shuttle bus to the trailhead at **Happy Isles.** (Or you can add 1 mi/1.6 km extra each way by hiking from the day-use parking area in Curry Village to Happy Isles.) The partially paved route is a moderate 500-foot (152-m) climb to the Vernal Fall **footbridge,** then a very steep tromp up the seemingly endless granite staircase to the top of the fall. Although many people hike only to the footbridge, 0.8 mile (1.3 km) from Happy Isles, it's definitely worth the extra effort to push on another 0.5 mile (0.8 km) to reach the top of **Vernal Fall.**

Climbing to the top means ascending another 500 feet (150 m) on the Mist Trail's famous **granite stairway,** which frames the edge of Vernal Fall. You will come so close to the plunging spray that you may feel as if you are part of it. Sometimes you are—during peak snowmelt in spring, hikers are frequently drenched in spray and mist. Remember to bring a rain poncho if you don't like getting wet. When you reach the 317-foot-high (97-m) fall's **brink,** you can stand at the railing and watch the dizzying flow of rushing white water as it tumbles downward. This is a trip you have to do at least once in your life.

After stopping at the Vernal Fall overlook, continue along the river's edge, passing a gorgeous stretch of stream known as the **Emerald Pool,** still following the Mist Trail. In 0.5 mile (0.8 km), the path crosses the river again and then climbs another mile (1.6 km) to the brink of **Nevada Fall.** Total elevation gain to the top of the 594-foot (181-m) falls is 2,600 feet (790 m), a healthy ascent. But when you get to walk this close to two world-class waterfalls, who's complaining? For your return trip, cross the **footbridge** above Nevada Fall and follow the **John Muir Trail** to loop back. As you descend, check out the great view of Nevada Fall with Liberty Cap in the background. This is one of the most memorable scenes in Yosemite Valley.

Note that you can cut back over to the Mist Trail at **Clark Point,** just above Vernal Fall, if you so desire. That way, you get a second chance to see Vernal Fall and hike the Mist Trail's granite staircase. But let your knees decide—plenty of hikers don't want to face those stairsteps a second time, especially in the downhill direction.

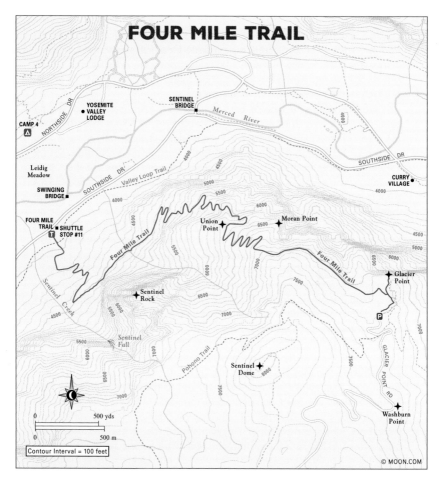

FOUR MILE TRAIL

DISTANCE: 9.6 miles (15.5 km) round-trip
DURATION: 5-6 hours
ELEVATION GAIN: 3,200 feet (975 m)
EFFORT: Strenuous
SHUTTLE STOP: 11
TRAILHEAD: Four Mile
DIRECTIONS: From the Arch Rock entrance station on Highway 140, drive 9.5 miles (15.3 km) east to the Four Mile Trailhead, next to mile marker V18 on the right side of Southside Drive. Park in the pullouts along the road.

Although the vast majority of Yosemite visitors get to Glacier Point by driving there, your arrival at this dramatic overlook is made more meaningful if you get there using your own power. That means hiking the Four Mile Trail all the way up from the Valley floor, gaining 3,200 feet (975 m) in 4.8 miles (7.7 km)—not 4 miles (6.4 km), as the name implies. The trail is partially shaded and makes a terrific day hike with an early-morning start. A bonus is that in the summer months, the snack stand on Glacier Point is open during the day, so you can hike to the top with a light day pack and then order

whatever you want for lunch. Go ahead, have the chili dog—the hike back is all downhill.

The trail is remarkably well graded, and surprisingly, sections of it are paved, or partially paved. After the first mile (1.6 km) or so, the trail breaks out from the trees and delivers nonstop views every step of the way. The big reward comes when you reach **Glacier Point,** where you have unobstructed views of just about every major landmark in Yosemite Valley.

Note that you'll see many more people hiking downhill on this trail than uphill; that's because they've ridden the tour bus to Glacier Point so that they can make the one-way hike back down to the valley floor. But honestly, this trail is much better in the uphill direction, as the amazing views unfold with every turn and twist in the trail.

HALF DOME

DISTANCE: 16 miles (26 km) round-trip

DURATION: 8-10 hours
ELEVATION GAIN: 4,800 feet (1,465 m)
EFFORT: Very strenuous
SHUTTLE STOP: 16
TRAILHEAD: Happy Isles
DIRECTIONS: From the Arch Rock entrance station on Highway 140, drive 11.6 miles (18.7 km) east to the day-use parking lot at Curry Village. Board the free Yosemite Valley shuttle bus to Happy Isles, stop number 16.

No argument about it, Half Dome is one of those "once in your life you gotta do it" hikes. Just be sure you know what you're in for before you set out on this epic trail. You're in for 16 miles (26 km) round-trip, a 4,800-foot (1,463-m) elevation gain, and a staggering amount of company.

When to Go: Half Dome's cables are usually in place only **late May to mid-October,** so that's the only time to attempt the trip.

Permits: During the summer, about 300 people a day make the trek to Half Dome's summit, a number that is strictly regulated by a permit

Four Mile Trail

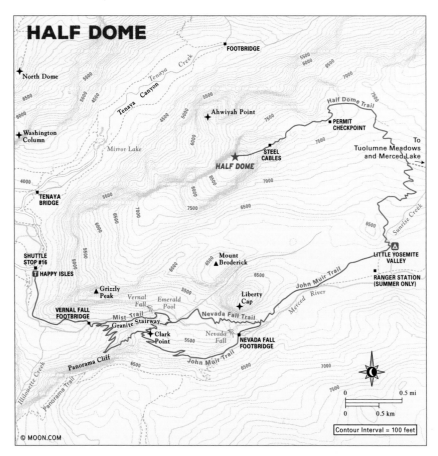

HALF DOME

FOOTBRIDGE

North Dome

Tenaya Creek

Tenaya Canyon

Washington Column

Ahwiyah Point

Mirror Lake

Half Dome Trail

PERMIT CHECKPOINT

To Tuolumne Meadows and Merced Lake

STEEL CABLES

HALF DOME

TENAYA BRIDGE

Sunrise Creek

SHUTTLE STOP #16

HAPPY ISLES

Mount Broderick

LITTLE YOSEMITE VALLEY

RANGER STATION (SUMMER ONLY)

Grizzly Peak

Vernal Fall

Emerald Pool

Liberty Cap

John Muir Trail

Merced River

VERNAL FALL FOOTBRIDGE

Mist Trail

Granite Stairway

Nevada Fall Trail

Clark Point

Nevada Fall

NEVADA FALL FOOTBRIDGE

Panorama Cliff

John Muir Trail

Illilouette Creek

Panorama Trail

0   0.5 mi

0   0.5 km

Contour Interval = 100 feet

© MOON.COM

system. The permits are designed to limit the amount of hiker traffic on Half Dome's famous cables. Most hikers make the trek as a day hike, but whether you do it in one day or opt for an overnight backpacking trip, you need to have a permit. Permits are acquired via two lottery processes. The **preseason lottery** takes place throughout the month of March, with results announced in mid-April (apply online at www. recreation.gov or by calling 877/444-6777). If you don't succeed in scoring a permit in March, you can try for the **daily lottery,** which takes place every day the cables are in place. Only 50 permits per day are given out in the daily lottery, and you must apply for a hiking permit two days in advance of your hike.

Planning: Plan on an early morning start to beat the heat and the possibility of afternoon clouds or thundershowers (**5am** is a common start time). Plan on not seeing your car again for 10-12 hours, during which time you must have everything you need in your day pack. Bring plenty of **water** and **food.** You'll be handing it out to others who are not so well prepared as well as gulping it down yourself. And consider carrying along a pair of **gloves** to keep your hands from slipping or chafing on the cables. (If you forget, you can

ascending Half Dome's cables

HALF DOME PERMITS

Permits are required to hike to the top of Half Dome. A maximum of 300 hikers are allowed per day on the Half Dome Trail beyond the granite formation known as Sub Dome. Of those 300 hikers, approximately 225 are day hikers and 75 are backpackers. Permits are distributed by lottery via www.recreation.gov. A preseason lottery, held in March, is supplemented by daily lotteries during the hiking season.

COSTS

A nonrefundable fee of $10 is charged when you submit an application. A second fee of $10 per person is charged only if you win the lottery and will receive a permit. Call for more information about daily Half Dome permits (209/372-0826; 9am-4:30pm Mon.-Fri. May-Sept.).

PRESEASON LOTTERY (MAR.)

Half Dome day hikers can apply for up to six permits (six people maximum). Each lottery application allows for a choice of up to seven dates. Hikers who choose dates that fall Monday-Thursday have a much better chance of winning than hikers who choose Friday-Sunday dates, when demand is much higher. Applications are taken online March 1-31 (www.recreation.gov). Lottery results are announced by email in mid-April.

How to Apply

On each application on www.recreation.gov, a trip leader and alternate trip leader must be designated. Each person may apply as a trip leader only once per lottery. (People applying multiple times as trip leader will have all their lottery applications canceled.) Preseason applications are successful if the number of permits requested are available on at least one of the requested dates. If permits are available for more than one of the requested dates, they are auto-

often find a discarded pair at the base of the cables, left by previous hikers.)

The Hike: Follow either the **John Muir Trail** or the **Mist Trail** from **Happy Isles** to the top of **Nevada Fall** (the Mist Trail is 0.6 mi/1 km shorter); then turn left and enter **Little Yosemite Valley,** where backpackers make camp. At 6.2 miles (10 km) the John Muir Trail splits off from the **Half Dome Trail;** head left for Half Dome.

Just under 2 miles (3.2 km) later you approach Half Dome's shoulder, which is a massive hump affectionately called **Sub Dome.** Here, during almost every single daylight hour, a **ranger** is stationed to make sure that hikers have a permit (hikers without permits are not allowed beyond Sub Dome's base). From this point, a **granite stairway** consisting of about 600 steps leads up the dauntingly steep face of Sub Dome. The views

matically awarded to the highest priority date, as specified by the applicant. Permits are valid only if the trip leader or alternate leader is accompanying the group using the permits. The trip leader must carry a photo ID and show up together with the entire group at the base of Sub Dome, where rangers check for permits. Permits are not transferable. Any resale or auction of permits will make the permit null and void.

DAILY LOTTERY (MAY-OCT.)

Hikers who didn't enter or succeed in the preseason lottery can try their luck at the daily lottery. Approximately 50 day-hiking permits are available each day by lottery during the hiking season (May-Oct.). The lottery is open for 13 hours each day (midnight-1pm Pacific time). If you are trying for the daily lottery, you have a much better chance (56 percent) of winning the lottery on a weekday. Only 31 percent of hikers who try for a weekend day will get a permit.

How to Apply

To apply for a daily lottery permit, go to www.recreation.gov or call 877/444-6777. For the daily lottery you must apply online two days prior to your desired hiking date, and you will be notified of the lottery results late the same night. (So, to hike on Saturday, you would apply on Thursday and receive an email notification of results late Thursday night.) Results are also available online or by phone the next morning.

BACKPACKING

Hikers who want to climb Half Dome as part of an overnight trip need to follow a completely different process; they must obtain a wilderness permit (www.nps.gov/yose/planyourvisit/wpres.htm) for backpacking and request a Half Dome permit for hiking to the summit. Permits for overnight trips can be obtained up to 24 weeks in advance by filling out the online wilderness permit request form at www.yosemite.org.

are outstanding, though, so there is plenty of reason to stop and catch your breath. Then the trail descends a bit before reaching the **steel cables** that run 440 feet (134 m) up the back of Half Dome.

This is where many hikers start praying and wishing there weren't so many other hikers on the cables at the same time. Do some soul-searching before you begin the cable ascent—turning around is not a good option once you're halfway up, since you'll create a logjam. Pull on your gloves; you'll need them to protect your hands as you pull yourself up the cables. Arm strength as well as leg strength is required to haul yourself up 440 feet (134 m) of nearly vertical granite.

When you reach the top, the views are so incredible that you forget all about your exertion. There's plenty of room for everyone on top of Half

view of Liberty Cap and Nevada Fall along the John Muir Trail (left); Swinging Bridge along the Yosemite Valley bike path (right)

Dome; its vast, mostly flat surface covers about 13 acres (5 ha).

Backpack option: To make the trip easier, you can camp at **Little Yosemite Valley,** 4.7 miles (7.6 km) in (overnight wilderness permit required), and save the final ascent for the next day. The best part of

an overnight trip is that you can access the cables and the summit long before the day hikers arrive. Figure on a little over two hours of hiking from your Little Yosemite Valley campsite to the summit. Then just get up early and go. You'll enjoy a much more peaceful experience.

BACKPACKING

Although the hiking trails in Yosemite Valley are most heavily used by day hikers, several trails begin in the Valley and lead out of it to overnight camping destinations. Far and away the most popular of these is the busy trail from **Happy Isles.** Every day in summer, day hikers swarm the trail to Vernal and Nevada Falls, and many continue on for the long trek to Half Dome.

No matter where you decide to go, remember that if you want to strap on a backpack and spend the night in Yosemite's wilderness, you must have a **permit** (209/372-0740; www.nps.gov/yose/planyourvisit/wildpermits.htm). Backpackers must always use bear canisters to store their food

for overnight trips. Hanging food from trees is illegal in Yosemite.

HALF DOME

Backpackers can make the trip to Half Dome easier by splitting it into two days. A designated camp is located at **Little Yosemite Valley,** 4.7 miles (7.6 km) from the start and about 3.5 miles (5.6 km) from Half Dome's summit. Permit reservations for this trail are nearly impossible to come by in the summer months, so you need to plan early. A less crowded and perhaps more appealing option for Half Dome backpackers is to continue past this camp on the John Muir Trail—heading toward **Tuolumne Meadows**—or follow the other fork toward **Merced Lake.** Backpackers

are permitted to set up camp as long as they are at least 2 miles (3.2 km) from Little Yosemite Valley. Either one of these options offers lovely scenery, although of course they add time and distance to the next day's summit ascent.

SNOW CREEK TRAIL

If you want to get away from the crowds, take the Snow Creek Trail from the **Mirror Lake** area up and out of the Valley. Of all the pathways that ascend the Valley's high walls, this one is the steepest. It heads up switchbacks toward Snow Creek and then gains the north rim of the Valley near **North Dome** and **Basket Dome**. You must travel at least 4 miles (6.4 km) beyond the Yosemite Valley floor before camping.

YOSEMITE FALLS

Although you can't camp at the top of Yosemite Falls, you can take a backpack trip up the **Upper Yosemite Fall Trail,** visit the waterfall's exhilarating brink, and then continue on to **Eagle Peak, El Capitan,** or **North Dome.** As long as you are 4 miles (6.4 km) from the Yosemite Valley floor and 1 mile (1.6 km) from the top of Yosemite Falls, you can make camp.

BIKING

- -

★ YOSEMITE VALLEY BIKE PATH

12 miles (19.3 km)

You can start your bike tour of Yosemite Valley from just about anywhere. The bike path runs right past Yosemite Valley Lodge and Curry Village and parallels the stretch of Northside and Southside Drives that runs between the two lodging facilities. If you wish, you can make stops at the trailheads for Lower Yosemite Fall and Mirror Lake. If you are on a rental bike, you are not permitted to ride it down the hill from Mirror Lake; there are too many pedestrians in this area, and their safety is a concern. Go ahead and ride your bike up this hill, then park it in the bike rack and take a stroll around Mirror Lake. Then, walk your bike back down. When you reach the flat stretch at the bottom, go ahead and start pedaling.

One of the best lengths of the looping bike path is on the western end, where it crosses the picturesque **Swinging Bridge** over the Merced River and provides a straight-on view of billowing Yosemite Falls. Now, isn't this better than driving a car?

RENTALS

Yosemite Valley Lodge and **Curry Village Recreation Center** (209/372-1208 or 209/372-8323; 9am-5pm daily spring and fall; 8am-8pm daily summer) rent bikes for $30 per half-day or $40 per day. The rental bikes are cruiser models that anyone can ride, even if you haven't been on a bike in years. They have bikes for men, women, and children, plus bikes with trailers for the little ones ($55 per half day or $75 per full day), as well as baby strollers, wheelchairs, and electric scooters. Helmets come with all rentals.

WATER SPORTS

RAFTING
Merced River

On any warm early-summer day in Yosemite you can take a drive up to Glacier Point, look down over its mighty edge, and see a flotilla of rafters drifting lazily downstream on the Merced River. Lazily? Yes, indeed. This is not river rafting as most people think of it. "River meandering" would be a better term.

Still, rafting is one of the greatest ways to see Yosemite Valley in early summer, with no traffic jams and no need for constant vigilance over oblivious pedestrians. Rafting is a matter of simply lying on your back, trailing a few fingers in the water, and gazing up at the granite walls as you float by. Sadly, the rafting season in Yosemite Valley is painfully short—typically **June-July**. The water level isn't usually low enough to be safe until **late May or early June,** and the season ends when the river gets too low and the rafts start scraping the river bottom, which is usually in late July.

rafting the Merced River

If you have your own inflatable raft or inner tube, you can bring it to the park and float on your own 10am-6pm daily. For $5, you can catch the shuttle back to your starting point. Whether you rent a raft or inner tube or bring your own, life jackets are mandatory. While you're out on the water, remember to protect the beautiful Merced River. If you choose to disembark, do so only on sandy beaches or gravel bars. Stay away from vegetated stream banks to protect the delicate riparian habitat.

Rentals

**CURRY VILLAGE
RECREATION CENTER**
209/372-4386; www.travelyosemite. com; 10am-4pm daily; rafts hold 2-4 people, $30.50 per person
Inflatable rafts can be rented at Curry Village Recreation Center; the put-in point is nearby. Rental rafts come complete with mandatory life jackets and paddles. You float 3 miles (4.8 km) downstream and then ride a shuttle bus back to your starting point. The whole adventure takes 3-4 hours. Children under 50 pounds (23 kg) are not permitted on rafts. If you have your own float but didn't bring a life jacket, you can rent one for $5.50 per person.

SWIMMING
Avoid spring and early summer, when swimming anywhere in the Merced River is a very bad idea—the current can be much stronger than it looks. The same is true for the pools above Vernal and Nevada Falls, Illilouette Fall, and Upper Yosemite Fall.

swimming in the Merced River

Although the water looks tempting after a hot and sweaty hike, even in late summer the current above these waterfalls can be deceptively swift—even deadly.

Merced River

From **mid-July to late September,** plenty of swimming holes can be found along the Merced River's sandy beaches on the Valley's east end, especially near Housekeeping Camp and the Pines campgrounds in an area called **Sentinel Beach.** The sandy bars found here are ideal for lounging along the river and are also the most ecologically sound spots for entering and exiting the water. In the interest of protecting the Merced's fragile shoreline, always stay off grassy meadow areas.

ROCK CLIMBING

CLIMBS

Be aware that the few "easier grade" climbs in Yosemite are quite popular. If you don't start early in the morning, you may be forced to wait in line. The greatest numbers of climbers hit the Valley in May and then again in September-October. The walls are less crowded in the summer when the temperatures are high.

Experienced climbers visiting the Valley for the first time should head for the **Royal Arches** (just east of The Ahwahnee), the southeast face of **Half Dome,** and a climb known as **Munginella** near Yosemite Falls. These climbs are mostly rated 5.6 and 5.7, but many find them more difficult than their ratings indicate. **El Capitan** is *definitely* not recommended for first-timers, or even many "experienced" intermediate climbers, although El Cap has a few routes that are much easier than others.

Yosemite Mountaineering School and Guide Service

Mountain Shop at Curry Village; 209/372-8344; www.travelyosemite. com; classes 8:30am daily mid-Apr.-Oct.; $195-440

If you don't have experience with granite crack climbing or traditional climbing, you might want to consider utilizing Yosemite Mountaineering School and Guide Service, which conducts seminars and classes for beginning, intermediate, and advanced climbers; equipment rentals are available. Private guided climbs lasting 6-10 hours are also available ($380 per person for individuals or $195 per person for groups of three).

BOULDERING

Those who enjoy bouldering will find plenty of it on the rocks around Camp 4. Other popular bouldering areas are found near **Cathedral Rocks** (directly across from El Capitan, on the south side of the Valley and just east of Bridalveil Fall) and The Ahwahnee.

CLIMB-WATCHING
El Capitan Meadow

If you'd rather watch rock climbers than be a rock climber, congratulate yourself on your levelheadedness and head to El Capitan Meadow, where with a pair of binoculars you can watch the slow progress of

climbers heading up the face of El Capitan. Ever since this 3,593-foot (1,095-m) rock face was conquered in the 1950s, bold successors have inched their way to the top. Most take anywhere between three and five days to do so; they spend their nights sleeping on ledges or tethered into hammocks.

Swan Slab
between the Lower Yosemite Fall parking lot and Camp 4
Swan Slab across from Yosemite Valley Lodge is another good place to watch climbers strut their stuff.

WINTER SPORTS

- -

SNOWSHOEING
Mirror Lake
Yosemite Valley doesn't always have enough snow for snowshoeing. Some years there's barely a dusting; other years, like the winter of 2023, there's several feet. You may have to carry your snowshoes as you walk up the paved road to the lake and then strap them on when you hit the trail. A 4-mile (6.4-km) loop can be made from Mirror Lake up Tenaya Canyon (see Mirror Lake Loop hike, page 58). It's a delightful surprise to see this area when it's peaceful, serene, and snow-covered (compared to the summer when it's packed with sightseers).

Rentals and Tours
Snowshoe rentals are available at the **Mountain Shop at Curry Village** (9am-5pm daily; $24 half day, $28.50 full day). If you don't want to snowshoe by yourself, check the free Yosemite newspaper for guided events. In the winter months, park

snowshoeing

rangers or naturalists often lead **snowshoe walks.**

ICE-SKATING
Curry Village Ice-Skating Rink
209/372-8210; daily late Nov.-Mar., weather permitting; $16 adults, $15 children

The original Curry Village skating rink had a long history in Yosemite Valley. It was started in 1928 by the Yosemite Park and Curry Company. The current rink, which first opened in winter 2016, is modular and can be easily removed when the season is over. Sessions are held in the afternoons and evenings on weekdays and from morning until evening on weekends. **Ice skate rentals** ($5.25) are available, and helmets are free on request. If you find yourself falling down more often than performing graceful pirouettes, head for the warming hut's fire pit and snack stand and treat yourself to a cup of hot chocolate.

FOOD

Without fail, the busiest locations in Yosemite Valley are the places that serve food. Judging from the lines out the door of most of the Valley's dining establishments, you might think that people came to this national park just to grab a meal. Or perhaps the lines are due to Yosemite's sweet mountain air making visitors hungry.

The Valley offers a wide range of food choices, and four central areas of the Valley serve food in either sit-down or carryout form: Yosemite Valley Lodge, Yosemite Village, Curry Village, and The Ahwahnee. If you're visiting in the summer season, you'll find that most food establishments are open only until 9pm. For current hours of operation for all the in-park restaurants, call 209/372-1001 (hours change seasonally).

STANDOUTS
The Village Grill
shuttle stop 2; 11am-8pm daily Apr.-Oct.; $8-15

The Village Grill serves fast-food items with no indoor seating, but there's nothing quite like having a

The Village Grill (left); Mountain Room (right)

Village Grill milk shake on the outdoor deck on a hot summer day.

Mountain Room
Yosemite Valley Lodge, shuttle stop 7; 209/372-1274 or 209/372-1403; 5pm-10pm daily; $22-45

The Mountain Room is the fanciest of a handful of dining choices at Yosemite Valley Lodge. The modern, sit-down restaurant serves classic entrées like steaks, seafood, chicken, and pasta dishes. Try to get a table near the windows so you can enjoy the spectacular Valley views. If you have dinner before dark, you can gaze up at Lower Yosemite Fall while you eat. Diners show up wearing everything from high heels to hiking boots, so come as you are. Try the mountain trout, ahi tuna, or tequila shrimp. Vegetarians can always find a pasta dish to suit their tastes. Everything on the menu is à la carte, so if you order an appetizer, an entrée, and dessert, you can easily spend $150 for two people without even opening the wine list. But you're on vacation, right? A welcome new change is that the Mountain Room now accepts reservations, which has made dining here even more enjoyable. You don't have to put your name on a list and wait two hours; simply reserve in advance at www.opentable.com.

The Ahwahnee Dining Room
The Ahwahnee, shuttle stop 3; 209/372-1489; 7am-10am, 11:30am-3pm, and 5:30pm-9pm daily; $35-50

If you like formality and have money to blow, don't hesitate for even a moment: Get a reservation for dinner at The Ahwahnee Dining Room. Ties and jackets are certainly apropos for this elegant restaurant, but in recent years the hotel has slackened its dress code to "resort casual," meaning that men should wear collared shirts and long pants, and women should wear dresses, skirts, or slacks and blouses. No jeans, tennis shoes, or T-shirts are permitted. Considering the quality of the food and the accompanying astronomical prices, formal attire seems fitting here. If you're dying to eat at The Ahwahnee but you're not the dress-up type, show up for breakfast or lunch, when even shorts and hiking boots will gain you entrance to the grand dining room.

Just how grand is it? The dining room fills a space 130 feet (40 m) long and has towering 37-foot-high (11-m) ceilings, and 400 people can eat dinner under its open-beamed roof all at once, with plenty of room to spare. It contains dozens of wrought-iron chandeliers and enormous picture windows that look out on classic Valley scenery.

Best of all, the food tastes as good as the dining room looks. The menu changes constantly, but certain well-loved items show up frequently, like salmon stuffed with Dungeness crab. In recent years the chef has placed a greater emphasis on organic and sustainably harvested ingredients, creating signature dishes such as pan-roasted, line-caught halibut and grilled wild king salmon. A children's menu is available.

The hotel's lavish Sunday **brunch** (7am-3pm Sun.; $56 adults, $22.50 children) is legendary. **Breakfast** (7am-10am Mon.-Sat.) and **lunch** (11:30am-3pm Mon.-Sat.) are not only the most casual meals of the day, they are also the most affordable ($16-32). Keep in mind that if you want to eat any meal other than

YOSEMITE VALLEY FOOD

NAME	LOCATION	TYPE
Degnan's Kitchen	Yosemite Village (shuttle stop 2)	sit-down
★ The Village Grill	Yosemite Village (shuttle stop 2)	takeout
Meadow Grill	Curry Village (shuttle stops 14 and 19)	takeout
Pizza Patio	Curry Village (shuttle stops 14 and 19)	takeout
Bar 1899	Curry Village (shuttle stops 14 and 19)	sit-down
Seven Tents Pavilion	Curry Village (shuttle stops 14 and 19)	cafeteria-style
Coffee Corner	Curry Village (shuttle stops 14 and 19)	takeout
★ Mountain Room	Yosemite Valley Lodge (shuttle stop 7)	sit-down
Mountain Room Lounge	Yosemite Valley Lodge (shuttle stop 7)	sit-down
Base Camp Eatery	Yosemite Valley Lodge (shuttle stop 7)	cafeteria-style
★ The Ahwahnee Dining Room	The Ahwahnee (shuttle stop 3)	sit-down
The Ahwahnee Bar	The Ahwahnee (shuttle stop 3)	sit-down

breakfast at The Ahwahnee, **reservations are a must.**

BEST PICNIC SPOTS
Church Bowl Picnic Area
Ahwahnee Hotel access road, 0.25 mile (0.4 km) west of shuttle stop 3

If you're looking to picnic somewhere far from the Valley's summer crowds, this is your best bet. Church Bowl is tucked out of the way on the access road to The Ahwahnee and Yosemite's medical clinic—a road that most Valley visitors don't drive since it's off the Northside-Southside Drive loop. The picnic area offers great views of Sentinel Rock and the cliffs below Glacier Point, and it's near a few popular rock climbing and bouldering sites, so you may get some free entertainment. Another big bonus: This picnic area has drinking water and flush toilets.

FOOD	PRICE	HOURS
sandwiches and baked goods	budget	7am-6pm daily summer, 7am-5pm daily winter
burgers and fast food	budget	11am-8pm daily Apr.-Oct.
burgers and fast food	budget	11am-6pm daily Apr.-Sept.
pizza	budget	noon-9pm daily summer
beer	budget	11am-9pm daily year-round
casual American	budget	7am-10am and 5:30pm-8pm daily
coffee, ice cream, snacks	budget	6:30am-11am daily summer
classic American	splurge	5pm-10pm daily
light meals and drinks	moderate	4pm-9pm Mon.-Fri., noon-9pm Sat.-Sun.
casual American	budget	6:30am-9pm daily
contemporary American	splurge	7am-10am, 11:30am-3pm, and 5:30pm-9pm daily
light meals and drinks	moderate	7am-10am and 11am-9pm daily

Lower Yosemite Fall Picnic Area
shuttle stop 6

This is the busiest picnic area in all of Yosemite, and it's not surprising considering it's located by the Lower Yosemite Fall Trailhead and it has drinking water and flush toilets. It's not easy to score a table here, but if you do, you can have a picnic lunch after or before strolling to the falls.

El Capitan Picnic Area
off Northside Drive, 1.2 miles (1.9 km) west of Camp 4, shuttle stop 8

Despite this picnic area's name, you can't see El Capitan from here, but that's only because you're right at its base. But if you're looking for a lovely woodsy spot to claim your own picnic table and charcoal grill, this is your best chance—El Capitan Picnic Area is one of the largest of the Valley picnic areas, with ample parking and

Lower Yosemite Fall Picnic Area

Church Bowl Picnic Area (left); Upper Pines Campground (right)

amenities. It's easy to take the short walk into El Cap Meadow to watch the climbers.

Sentinel Beach Picnic Area
access road off Southside Drive, 1 mile (1.6 km) east of Cathedral Beach, shuttle stop 11

When you pull into the parking area for Sentinel Beach Picnic Area, it doesn't look terribly promising. A few picnic tables and grills are scattered around a wide clearing of recently logged forest. But walk a short distance to the beach on the Merced River, and you'll see why this is one of the best places in Yosemite Valley to spread out a blanket or set up your lawn chairs and have a riverside lunch. There's a lovely view of Yosemite Falls, and the river is shallow and wide, perfect for wading youngsters.

Cathedral Beach Picnic Area
access road off Southside Drive, east of El Capitan Crossover, shuttle stop 10

For a drop-dead gorgeous view of El Capitan, it's tough to beat Cathedral Beach Picnic Area. Located at a kink in the Merced River that's away from the Valley's busy roads, this is a prime choice for families looking to wade or float in the river before or after a picnic lunch. It's also a great spot for couples who just want a shady spot where they can look up and admire the hulking profile of El Cap.

Cascades Picnic Area
Highway 140, 2.8 miles (4.5 km) east of the Arch Rock entrance

This picnic area on Highway 140 near El Portal is a good distance west of "central" Yosemite Valley, which means for most people it's a stopover on the way in or out of the park. And when the waterfall known as The Cascades is flowing in the spring months, no one can resist stopping here. Your kids can climb around on big granite boulders and enjoy the buzz of negative ions swirling through the air while you fill up your Instagram account with pretty Yosemite pictures. And of course you can picnic here too.

YOSEMITE VALLEY CAMPGROUNDS

NAME	LOCATION	SEASON
Upper Pines	near Curry Village (shuttle stop 15)	year-round
North Pines	near Curry Village (shuttle stop 15)	end of Mar.–mid-Oct. or early Nov.
Lower Pines	near Curry Village (shuttle stop 15)	end of Mar.–mid-Oct. or early Nov.
Camp 4	Northside Drive near Yosemite Valley Lodge (shuttle stop 7)	year-round

CAMPING

If you have your heart set on camping in Yosemite Valley, one of the most scenic places on earth, you'd better be one of those people who can plan far in advance. Simply put, these sites are in high demand. For the summer vacation season, every reservable site in Yosemite Valley is snatched up as soon as it shows up in the reservation system. Contact **Recreation.gov** (877/444-6777 or 518/885-3639 from outside the U.S. and Canada; www.recreation.gov) up to **five months in advance** in order to reserve a site at one of three reservable campgrounds (Upper Pines, North Pines, and Lower Pines) in Yosemite Valley. Reservations are available in blocks of one month at a time, on the **15th of each month starting at 7am** Pacific time. Both the telephone and the online reservation systems are open 7am-7pm Pacific time daily November-February, and 7am-9pm Pacific

SITES AND AMENITIES	RV LIMIT	PRICE	RESERVATIONS
238 tent and RV sites; drinking water and flush toilets; accessible sites available	up to 40 feet (12 m) long	$36	yes
81 tent and RV sites; drinking water and flush toilets; accessible sites available	up to 35 feet (10.7 m) long	$36	yes
60 tent and RV sites; drinking water and flush toilets; accessible sites available	up to 40 feet (12 m) long	$36	yes
36 walk-in tent sites; drinking water and flush toilets; accessible sites available	no RVs	$10 pp	yes

time daily March–October. Even with a reservation, it's wise to show up right around checkout time (10am or earlier) so that you can have your pick of available sites as campers vacate their spots. With your reservation, you are guaranteed a site, but you are not guaranteed a *good* site.

With all these hoops to jump through, you'd think that the campgrounds in Yosemite Valley would be fabulous. The truth is, they're not. If you think camping should feel like a real "nature experience," you've come to the wrong place.

The Valley's campsites are so close together that you'll feel like your neighbors are sharing your vacation with you. You'll hear the sound of cars driving around the campgrounds and nearby roads all night.

You'll also spend a fair portion of your camping time engaged in the business of "taking bear precautions." This means, first and foremost, that you do not store any food, or any item with a scent (including cosmetics, sunscreen, lip balm, toothpaste, and insect repellent) in your car or tent. Everything with a scent gets

YOSEMITE VALLEY LODGING

NAME	LOCATION	SEASON
Housekeeping Camp	Southside Drive (shuttle stop 12)	Apr.–Oct.
Curry Village	Southside Drive (shuttle stops 14 and 20)	year-round
Yosemite Valley Lodge	Northside Drive (shuttle stop 8)	year-round
★ The Ahwahnee	The Ahwahnee (shuttle stop 3)	year-round

placed in your campsite's metal bear box, including your cooler filled with food and ice. Most bear boxes are 33 inches (84 cm) deep, 45 inches (114 cm) wide, and 18 inches (46 cm) high, so make sure you don't have more stuff than will cram into that space.

LODGING

Of the seven lodgings available inside the park boundaries, four are in Yosemite Valley—the marvelous but pricey Ahwahnee, the mid-priced Yosemite Valley Lodge, and the budget but bare-bones Curry Village and Housekeeping Camp.

RESERVATIONS

Reservations for park lodgings inside Yosemite are made by phone through Aramark's **Yosemite Hospitality** (888/413-8869, 7am-5pm Mon.-Fri., 8am-5pm Sat.-Sun. summer, shorter hours in winter) or online (www.travelyosemite.com). For stays from late April to mid-October and during winter holidays, it is wise to make reservations **up to a year in advance.** Cancellations happen frequently, so if you strike out, keep calling back. During the off-season it is not terribly difficult to get a room, even in Yosemite Valley, particularly midweek. A few days' notice should be all you need, except during holiday periods.

STANDOUTS
The Ahwahnee
shuttle stop 3; 888/413-8869; www.travelyosemite.com; $425-590 in summer, less in winter
If a wad of bills is burning a hole in your pocket, book a stay at The Ahwahnee.

Built in 1927, The Ahwahnee is a National Historic Landmark designed by Gilbert Stanley Underwood. Its rooms are on the small side, as is typical of older hotels. But the views from its windows make up for any

OPTIONS	PRICE
duplex camp-style units with canvas roofs, privacy curtains, and shared baths	units from $108
motel rooms with private baths, wooden cabins with private and shared baths, tent cabins with shared baths	rooms from $196, wooden cabins from $230, tent cabins from $160
motel rooms with private baths	rooms from $227
hotel rooms, cottages, two-room suites	rooms from $425

shortcomings in square footage. One side of the hotel faces Glacier Point and Half Dome. The other side faces Yosemite Falls. The higher the room, the better the view, so be sure to request a spot on the 4th, 5th, or 6th floors. If you have an unlimited budget, reserve one of the handful of ultra-pricy two-room suites on the top floor. Another great option: Book one of the 24 cozy private cottages in the forest behind the hotel. Two of the most coveted cottages have fireplaces.

Make sure you book early. Even with its sky-high prices, The Ahwahnee is often full.

Even if you don't sleep or eat here,

tent cabins at Curry Village

be sure to visit The Ahwahnee's several "public rooms." Wandering through this grand hotel's lobby and sitting rooms gives you the chance to marvel at the hotel's architecture, including massive hand-stenciled timber beams, sandstone fireplaces, and colorful stained-glass windows. Adorning this venerable structure are Native American tapestries and baskets, Turkish kilim rugs, and Yosemite-inspired art such as Gunnar Widforss's 19th-century paintings depicting the park's waterfalls and giant sequoias. Take a walk around the **Great Lounge,** and buy a drink at the bar or a souvenir in one of the gift shops. Free one-hour guided **tours** of The Ahwahnee are offered throughout the year; check with the hotel's concierge desk for a current schedule.

The Ahwahnee

INFORMATION AND SERVICES

Yosemite Village, home to the Valley Welcome Center, a huge general goods store, and a post office, is the main hub for services in the park. Nearby **Curry Village** has a few services, including an outdoor gear shop and a small grocery store. **Yosemite Lodge** also has a small general goods store.

Entrance Stations

Arch Rock Entrance

Highway 140

Arch Rock, only a 15- to 20-minute drive, is the closest entrance station to Yosemite Valley. Arch Rock is the popular year-round entrance to the park and provides access to Yosemite Valley from the west.

Big Oak Flat Entrance

Highway 120

Big Oak Flat offers access from the north; it's about a 45-minute drive to Yosemite Valley.

Visitor Centers

Valley Welcome Center

shuttle stop 1; 209/372-0299; 9am-5pm daily year-round

The largest of the park's visitor centers is located in Yosemite Valley, and as of 2023, has a brand-new building. The 3,000-square-foot (279-square-meter) building next to the Yosemite Village Store replaced the Valley Visitor Center that had operated since 1967. Located much closer to Yosemite Village's central parking lot, the new Welcome Center features educational displays, restrooms, and a 20,000-square-foot (1,858-square-meter) outdoor plaza. Park rangers and Yosemite Conservancy volunteers help visitors plan their trips, and free day-hiking brochures are available.

An exhibit hall interprets the geologic history of Yosemite Valley and explains park wildlife and how it adapts to the Sierra Nevada's seasonal changes. A 23-minute National Park Service-sanctioned film, *The Spirit of Yosemite,* is shown in the **Valley Welcome Center Theater** on the half hour starting at 9:30am daily except Sunday, when the first showing is at noon. The film explains some of the basics about Yosemite's geology and history but mostly consists of a lot of beautiful videography.

Happy Isles Art and Nature Center

shuttle stop 16; 9am-4pm daily Apr.-Oct.

A lesser-known visitor center is the Happy Isles Art and Nature Center. This small interpretive center has family-oriented exhibits on the natural history and geology of the Valley, including wildlife dioramas and interactive displays. Short nature trails lead from the center, including one that explores evidence of a massive 1996 landslide that completely devastated this region of the park. Art classes for kids and adults are offered daily. Register online (www.yosemite.org) to secure a spot, or show up at 9:30am for last-minute openings. They also host open studio workshop hours (11am-3pm daily Apr.-Oct.). Classes are held outside when weather permits. Happy Isles is also the trailhead for the famous hikes to Vernal and Nevada Falls and Half Dome.

TRANSPORTATION

Getting There

Please note that drive times vary widely according to traffic conditions. A one-hour drive can easily become a two-or three-hour drive (or longer) on a Saturday or Sunday in July or August, especially when there is a line-up of cars at the park entrance station.

From Arch Rock Entrance

Yosemite Valley is 15 miles (24 km) east of the Arch Rock Entrance, about a 20-minute drive. From the entrance, continue on Highway 140/El Portal Road until the road splits into one-way Southside and Northside Drives. Southside Drive heads east, and the main sights in the Valley start

past the El Capitan crossover. To reach Yosemite Village, stay on Southside Drive and turn left on Sentinel Drive, which leads to the main Yosemite Village parking lot.

From Big Oak Flat Entrance

From the northern Big Oak Flat Entrance on Highway 120, the 24-mile (39-km) drive to Yosemite Valley takes about 45 minutes. From the entrance, continue on Big Oak Flat Road until it merges with Highway 140/El Portal Road. After a few miles, the road splits into Southside and Northside Drives. Take Southside Drive into the Valley.

From Glacier Point

From Glacier Point, take Glacier Point Road 16 miles (26 km) west to Chinquapin junction. Make a right onto Wawona Road/Highway 41, and it's a 14-mile (22.5-km) drive north to Yosemite Valley. This drive takes about 55 minutes but may be longer if traffic is heavy.

From Wawona

From Wawona, Yosemite Valley is 29 miles (46.5 km) north on Wawona Road/Highway 41. This drive takes about 50 minutes but may be longer if traffic is heavy.

From Tioga Road and Tuolumne Meadows

If you are driving to Yosemite Valley from Tioga Pass, plan on just under two hours to make the 62-mile (100-km) drive. Take Tioga Road through Tioga Pass, past Tuolumne Meadows, Tenaya Lake, and Olmsted Point to the western end of Tioga Road. At Crane Flat, turn left onto Big Oak Flat Road. From there, it's a 20-mile (32-km) drive south to the main lodgings and campgrounds in Yosemite Valley.

From Hetch Hetchy

From Hetch Hetchy Reservoir, Yosemite Valley is a 40-mile (64-km) drive. Take Hetch Hetchy Road (open 7am-9pm daily May-Labor Day, may be closed briefly during or just after winter storms) away from the reservoir for 7.5 miles (12 km) and pass through the Hetch Hetchy Entrance. From here, it's 1.5 miles (2.4 km) to Camp Mather, where you turn left (south) onto Evergreen Road (the road may be closed in winter). Drive south on Evergreen Road for about 7.5 miles (12.1 km) to Highway 120 and turn left (south). In 1 mile (1.6 km), drive through the Big Oak Flat Entrance, and it's another 24 miles (39 km) to Yosemite Valley. Plan on about 75 minutes to make this drive in good weather.

Parking

Parking is often difficult in Yosemite Valley in summer. If you are visiting Yosemite Valley May-September, consider leaving

your car in one of the day-use parking areas and riding the free shuttle bus or taking an organized tour. The main day-use parking lot is located south of the Yosemite Village Store, and there's another large lot at Curry Village. There are also parking lots at some attractions, including the Bridalveil Fall parking area, El Capitan Picnic Area, and Lower Yosemite Fall.

Gas and Charging

There is **no gas station** in Yosemite Valley. The closest gas station is outside the park in El Portal (12 mi/19.3 km). The closest gas inside the park is at **Crane Flat,** 15 mi (24 km) north on Big Oak Flat Road.

The only electric vehicle charging stations in the park are in Yosemite Valley and Tuolumne Meadows. You can charge your vehicle near the Village Store at the **Village Garage** (9002 Village Dr.; 209/372-8320; 8am-5pm daily), at **The Ahwahnee** (you do not need to be a guest to use this station) or **Yosemite Valley Lodge,** and just west of the Tuolumne Meadows Store. You can also charge your vehicle at **Rush Creek Lodge,** just 1.6 miles (2.6 km) west of Yosemite's Big Oak Flat entrance on Highway 120.

Shuttles

Free hybrid shuttle buses transport visitors around the Yosemite Valley floor year-round. To get a seat on one of these buses, simply stand at one of the shuttle stops and wait a few minutes until one shows up. If you're arriving in the Valley during the busy summer season, it is highly recommended that you park your car and use the free shuttles. All of the Valley's major sights are accessible via the shuttle.

Valleywide Shuttle

The main Valleywide shuttle runs 7am-10pm daily in summer, with shorter hours in winter. The shuttle visits each stop every 12 minutes during peak hours and every 22 minutes in the early morning and evening. The ride around the entire route takes one and a half hours.

East Valley Shuttle

The East Valley shuttle runs only about half the distance of the Valleywide shuttle, stopping only at points on the east end of Yosemite Valley, including Housekeeping Camp, Yosemite Village, Curry Village, Happy Isles, and The Ahwahnee. The shuttle operates 7am-10pm daily in summer, with shorter hours in winter, and visits each stop every 8-12 minutes. The ride around the entire route takes about 50 minutes.

Sentinel Dome

GLACIER POINT AND WAWONA

To the Native Americans who traveled between the foothills and Yosemite Valley, Wawona was the halfway point on their journey. They called it Pallachun, meaning "a good place to stay." This popular encampment later became the site of a wayside inn built by Galen Clark. Today it is home to the historic Wawona Hotel and a private community of homes, many of which can be rented by visitors. Now, as then, Wawona is a good place to stay.

It's also a good place to visit, with fishing and swimming holes in the South Fork Merced River, an excellent hiking trail to Chilnualna Falls, the natural spectacle of the Mariposa Grove of Giant Sequoias, and an opportunity to "step back in time" at the Pioneer Yosemite History Center. Plus, Wawona offers convenient access to Glacier Point, one of the grandest viewpoints in the West. The commanding vista from Glacier Point takes in all the major granite landmarks of Yosemite Valley and the surrounding high country. For many park visitors, it is Yosemite's single most memorable spot.

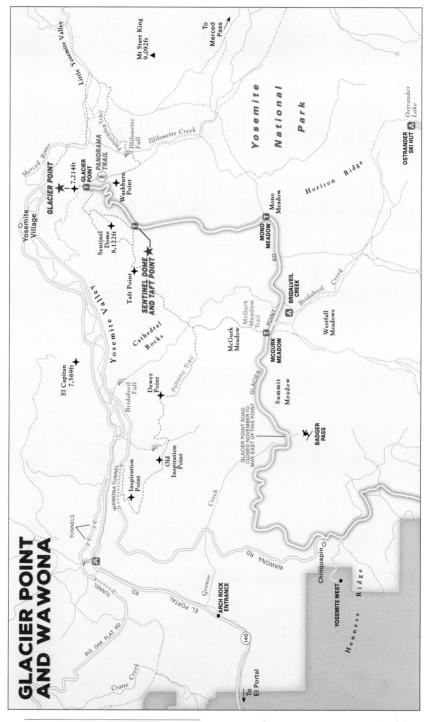

GLACIER POINT AND WAWONA

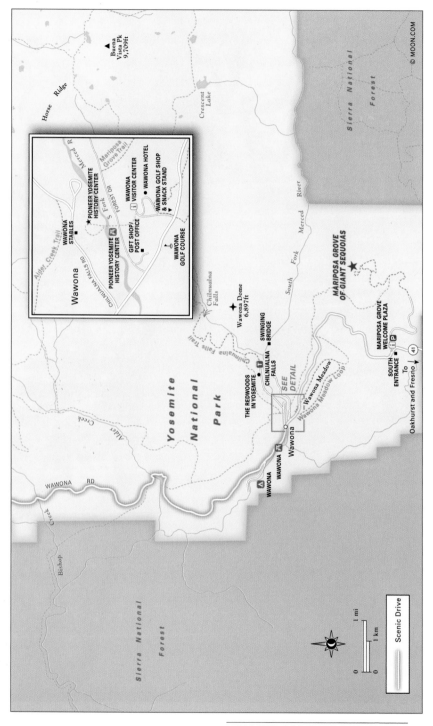

TOP 3

★ **1. GLACIER POINT:** This spectacular granite precipice overlooks Yosemite Valley, Half Dome, and the High Sierra. Come in the afternoon and stay for sunset (page 101).

★ **2. SENTINEL DOME AND TAFT POINT:** Two short hikes to these two overlook points start at the same trailhead. Both are short and easy enough for families (page 102).

★ **3. MARIPOSA GROVE OF GIANT SEQUOIAS:** See the largest living trees on earth by volume. Casual visitors can wander through the lower grove to see the most famous trees; more serious hikers can trek to the upper grove (page 103).

GLACIER POINT AND WAWONA 3 WAYS

HALF DAY

1 Follow Glacier Point Road to its end at **Glacier Point** to see the commanding vista from this 7,214-foot (2,199-m) granite precipice that lurches over Yosemite Valley and reveals a slew of park icons, including Half Dome, Clouds Rest, Liberty Cap, and Vernal and Nevada Falls. For many park visitors, this is Yosemite's single most photo-worthy spot.

2 As you drive away from Glacier Point, stop at **Washburn Point** (just 0.75 mi/1.2 km away) for an astonishing bird's-eye view of the High Sierra, including Vernal and Nevada Falls and the Merced River's "Grand Staircase" descending from the Clark Range.

3 Can't get enough eye candy? Indulge in more on the 1-mile (1.6-km) hike to **Sentinel Dome,** where you'll have a full 360-degree panorama that takes in many of the same landmarks seen from Glacier Point, with the addition of Yosemite Falls to the north.

4 Retrace your tire treads along Glacier Point Road and turn south on Highway 41, heading for Wawona. Stop for lunch at the 1879 **Wawona Hotel,** a white and green Victorian charmer with a covered veranda.

5 Next, head over to the **Mariposa Grove Welcome Plaza.** Board the shuttle for the 2-mile (3.2-km) drive to Yosemite's largest sequoia grove with more than 500 mature trees, each more than 10 feet (3 m) in diameter. Stroll through the lower grove and tilt your head way back to see super-size trees like the Grizzly Giant.

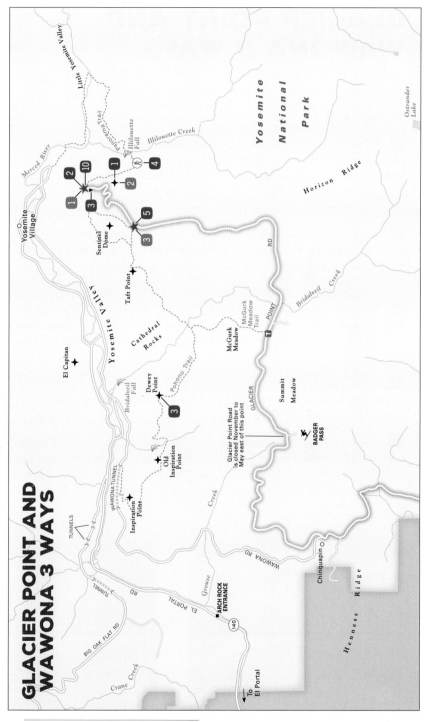

GLACIER POINT AND WAWONA 3 WAYS

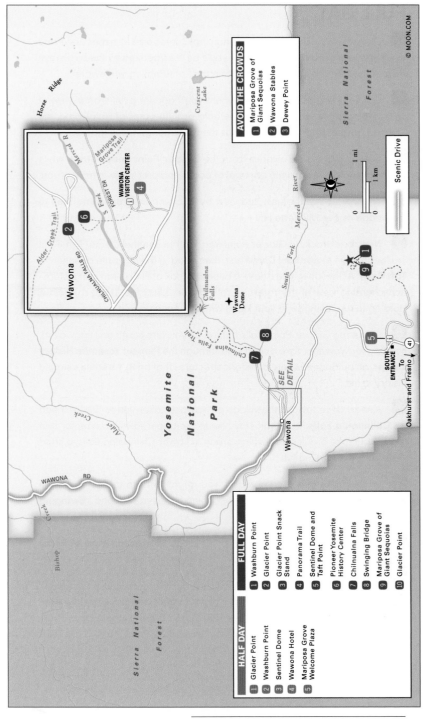

AVOID THE CROWDS

1 Mariposa Grove of
  Giant Sequoias
2 Wawona Stables
3 Dewey Point

Scenic Drive

1 mi
1 km

© MOON.COM

Horse Ridge

Crescent Lake

Mariposa Grove Trail

WAWONA VISITOR CENTER

Merced R

S Fork

FOREST DR

Wawona

CHILNUALNA FALLS RD

Alder Creek Trail

Yosemite National Park

Wawona Dome

Chilnualna Falls

Chilnualna Falls Trail

Merced River

South Fork

SEE DETAIL

Wawona

WAWONA RD

Alder Creek

Bishop Creek

Sierra National Forest

SOUTH ENTRANCE

To Oakhurst and Fresno

41

Sierra National Forest

HALF DAY

1 Glacier Point
2 Washburn Point
3 Sentinel Dome
4 Wawona Hotel
5 Mariposa Grove
  Welcome Plaza

FULL DAY

1 Washburn Point
2 Glacier Point
3 Glacier Point Snack
  Stand
4 Panorama Trail
5 Sentinel Dome and
  Taft Point
6 Pioneer Yosemite
  History Center
7 Chilnualna Falls
8 Swinging Bridge
9 Mariposa Grove of
  Giant Sequoias
10 Glacier Point

FULL DAY

1 Drive the winding ribbon of asphalt that curves past lush meadows and fir forests to **Washburn Point,** where you'll be mesmerized by the bird's-eye view of the Merced River's "Grand Staircase" of tumbling whitewater.

2 Continue on to **Glacier Point,** where you'll admire a full-frontal view of Yosemite's granite wonderland of the bald granite pates of Half Dome, the Quarter Domes, and Liberty Cap, plus the Clark Range far to the east.

3 Fuel up with some calories from the **Glacier Point Snack Stand** while you contemplate the granite banquet of peaks and precipices in front of you.

4 Then, walk *into* the postcard view by following the **Panorama Trail** to the bridge above Illilouette Fall.

5 Next, backtrack on Glacier Point Road to the Sentinel Dome/Taft Point Trailhead. Hike to **Sentinel Dome** first, then head in the opposite direction to **Taft Point.** At the latter, you'll have a head-on look at El Capitan and a stomach-churning view of the Yosemite Valley floor, 3,500 feet (1,100 m) below. Hold on to the railing (and your kids!) while you peer over it.

6 Leave the Glacier Point trails behind as you turn south on Highway 41, heading for Wawona. Take a short walk through the **Pioneer Yosemite History Center,** an outdoor museum of historic structures that bring Yosemite's storied history to life.

7 A short drive toward the village of Wawona takes you to the trailhead for **Chilnualna Falls.** It's a half-day hike to the upper falls—no time for that today—but take a quick, refreshing break at Lower Chilnualna Falls, a short walk from the parking lot.

8 While you're in a watery mood, you might want to take a dip in the South Fork Merced River. A favorite swimming hole is at Wawona's **Swinging Bridge.**

9 Reserve a couple of hours for a visit to the **Mariposa Grove of Giant Sequoias.** Even if time is running short, make sure you take the 1.6-mile (2.5-km) round-trip walk to the Grizzly Giant.

10 As your day nears its end, pack a picnic supper and drive back to **Glacier Point** in time for sunset and see Half Dome briefly turning pink. Then, after sundown, stick around to take part in the Glacier Point Starry Night Skies over Yosemite program.

AVOID THE CROWDS

1 You don't want to miss the **Mariposa Grove of Giant Sequoias,** but you'll enjoy the big trees much more if you visit them early in the morning or late in the day, when the grove is at its quietest. Try to arrive no later than 8am, or after 5pm, for the best experience. At any time of day, get away from the crowds by heading uphill to the more secluded upper grove.

2 Get into the Western spirit by climbing on a horse at **Wawona Stables** for a two- or four-hour ride. Make reservations ahead of time.

3 Along Glacier Point Road, the views at Taft Point and Sentinel Dome are deservedly popular, but if you put a few extra miles under your feet, you can get an equally astounding vista without the crowds by hiking to **Dewey Point** instead. Start at the McGurk Meadow Trailhead and walk 3.5 miles (5.6 km) to this spectacular promontory on the Valley's south rim.

HIGHLIGHTS

★ GLACIER POINT
end of Glacier Point Road

Often referred to as "the grandest view in all the West," Glacier Point is a 7,214-foot (2,199-m) overlook with a vista of Yosemite Valley, Half Dome and all its granite neighbors, and the High Sierra. The overlook area features a beautiful **amphitheater** for evening ranger talks, an imposing log cabin housing a **snack stand and gift shop** (summer only), and a large and clean restroom, plus all the historical highlights of the point: the stone-constructed **Geology Hut** that faces Half Dome, and the rock railings that look out over Vernal and Nevada Falls and the Merced River Canyon.

Glacier Point sees a lot of visitors all day long, especially in the peak summer months. If you want to nab a great spot to set up your tripod for sunset photos, plan to arrive about two hours before sunset. Even though Glacier Point faces east, away from the setting sun, the eastern sky lights up with pinks and golds. Half Dome is famous for turning pink for about 15 minutes each evening.

Sunset ranger programs (www. travelyosemite.com; 8pm) are held several nights each week in summer at the Glacier Point railing or amphitheater. Stargazing programs are held on clear Saturday nights. A telescope is set up for viewing the heavens. Scheduled events are posted at Glacier Point and online.

The **Glacier Point Starry Night Skies Over Yosemite Tour** (Sun.-Thurs. June-Sept.; $67 adults, $46.50 ages 5-12) departs Yosemite Valley Lodge at 7pm on summer evenings, arriving at Glacier Point just before dark. Tours last about four hours and a one-hour astronomy program takes place after dark. If

sunset on Half Dome as seen from Glacier Point

BEST PLACE TO WATCH THE SUNSET

Join the in-the-know visitors who show up at **Glacier Point** to see Half Dome blushing pink with alpenglow.

you're staying in the Wawona area, you can drive your own car to Glacier Point and pay $10 per person to participate in the one-hour stargazing program.

Sunrise is another lovely time to visit Glacier Point. Although the colors are not as dramatic as at sunset, you may have this entire beautiful overlook to yourself.

To reach Glacier Point from Wawona, drive 12 miles (19.3 km) north on Highway 41 and turn east onto Glacier Point Road. Continue 15 miles (24 km) east on Glacier Point Road to the parking lot; it's about a 400-foot (120-m) walk to the overlook. From Yosemite Valley, drive 9 miles (14.5 km) south on Wawona Road to reach the Glacier Point turnoff.

WASHBURN POINT
Glacier Point Road, 0.75 mile (1.2 km) south of Glacier Point (parking area on the left when heading south)
Many visitors bypass this overlook in their hurry to get to Glacier Point, but Washburn Point is worth a stop in its own right. Washburn Point offers a dizzying perspective of Half Dome and the granite country of the High Sierra. Although you won't see much of Yosemite Valley, it has the best possible view of Vernal and Nevada Falls. The overlook was named for the Washburn brothers, who owned the original Wawona Hotel and drove visitors by stagecoach to this spot in the 1870s.

★ SENTINEL DOME AND TAFT POINT
Glacier Point Road, about 2 miles (3.2 km) south of Glacier Point
These two spectacular overlooks cannot be seen from the car, but if

the outstanding view from the summit of Sentinel Dome (left); cabin at the Pioneer Yosemite History Center (right)

you have the time and energy, either destination will round out your trip to Glacier Point. Sentinel Dome, a granite dome topping out at 8,122 feet (2,476 m), offers a breathtaking view of Yosemite Falls and a 360-degree panorama of granite peaks and domes. The view from Taft Point is completely different: a head-on look at El Capitan and a stomach-churning view of the Yosemite Valley floor, 3,500 feet (1,100 m) below. Hold on to the railing (and your children) while you peer over it. Both trails lead from the same parking lot but head in opposite directions; each requires a hike of 1.1 miles (1.8 km) one-way. For more information on these two short hiking destinations, see the Best Hikes section (page 107).

PIONEER YOSEMITE HISTORY CENTER

Wawona

The Pioneer Yosemite History Center brings Yosemite's history to life. These historic buildings, many of which were relocated from other places in the park to this collection, are from different periods of Yosemite's history—a **U.S. Cavalry office,** a **Wells Fargo station** that served stagecoach passengers, a **jail,** and a few homesteads. Live demonstrations are often held at the **blacksmith shop** and other buildings (check the Yosemite newspaper for dates and times). **Horse-drawn carriage rides** (10 minutes, $7 adults, $4 ages 3-12) are offered daily. You can walk around the buildings' exteriors on your own (an interpretive brochure is available); in the summer months, docents sometimes dress in period costumes and lead visitors on free tours inside the buildings.

To reach the Pioneer Yosemite History Center, cross Forest Drive and walk through a **covered bridge** across the South Fork Merced River. The bridge was built in 1857 by the Washburn brothers, who established a tourist facility in what later became Wawona. The Washburn brothers owned the Wawona Hotel and most of the land in this area until 1932, when the National Park Service purchased it.

★ MARIPOSA GROVE OF GIANT SEQUOIAS

The Mariposa Grove is the largest grove of sequoias in the park. Its 250 acres (100 ha) contain more than 500 mature trees, each more than 10 feet (3 m) in diameter, as well as hundreds of smaller trees. The grove is divided into two areas—upper and lower. Most casual visitors stroll through the lower grove to see the most famous "named" trees, like the 3,000-year-old Grizzly Giant, Yosemite's largest tree at 210 feet (64 m) tall and 29 feet (9 m) in diameter. Adventurous hikers will want to wander around both the upper and lower groves to Wawona Point, a 7-mile (11.3-km) round-trip with a substantial amount of climbing (about 1,200 ft/365 m).

The main 300-car parking lot, named the Mariposa Grove Welcome Plaza, is located 2 miles (3.2 km) away from the grove, near the park's South entrance. Most of the year, visitors can access the grove only by walking or riding a shuttle bus from the Welcome Plaza. To visit the Mariposa Grove April-November, take one of the free **shuttle buses** (every 10-15 minutes 8am-8pm daily Apr. 1-Sept. 7, 8am-5:30pm daily late fall) from the Welcome Plaza. If you arrive very early in the morning,

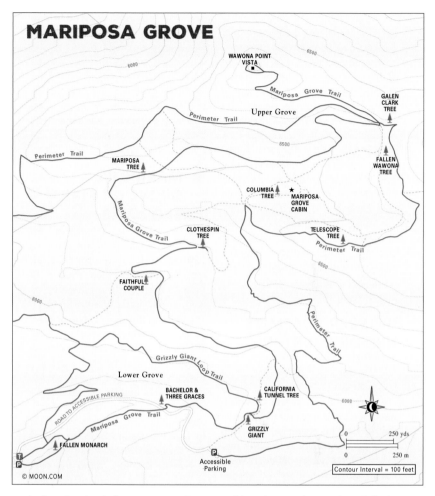

MARIPOSA GROVE

WAWONA POINT VISTA

6500

6000

Mariposa Grove Trail

Upper Grove

GALEN CLARK TREE

Perimeter Trail

6500

Perimeter Trail

MARIPOSA TREE

FALLEN WAWONA TREE

COLUMBIA TREE

★ MARIPOSA GROVE CABIN

Mariposa Grove Trail

CLOTHESPIN TREE

TELESCOPE TREE

Perimeter Trail

6500

FAITHFUL COUPLE

6000

Perimeter Trail

Grizzly Giant Loop Trail

Lower Grove

BACHELOR & THREE GRACES

CALIFORNIA TUNNEL TREE

6000

ROAD TO ACCESSIBLE PARKING

Mariposa Grove Trail

GRIZZLY GIANT

0   250 yds

FALLEN MONARCH

0   250 m

Accessible Parking

Contour Interval = 100 feet

© MOON.COM

before the shuttle buses are running, you may be able to drive your own car into the grove; about two dozen parking spots are available at the trailhead. If you have a disabled placard for your car, you can drive in at any time. From December to March, shuttles do not run, but visitors can park in the lot near Highway 41 and snowshoe or walk along the road into the grove.

Lower Grove

Many visitors choose to visit only some of the more "famous" trees by walking the 2-mile (3.2-km) **Grizzly Giant Loop** that starts at the Arrival Area and passes the Bachelor and Three Graces, Fallen Monarch, the Grizzly Giant, and the California Tunnel Tree. Interpretive signs on the trail to the Grizzly Giant provide an informative self-guided tour.

The **Fallen Monarch,** which fell more than 300 years ago, was made famous by an 1899 photograph of U.S. Cavalry troopers and their horses standing on top of it. A short walk east from the parking lot is the **Grizzly Giant,** the largest tree

in this grove at 210 feet (64 m) tall and 31 feet (9.4 m) across at its base. The most photographed sequoia in Yosemite, this behemoth is about 1,800 years old. Its massive, gnarled branches appear to be sculpted by some unseen hand. One particularly impressive branch measures almost 7 feet (2 m) in diameter—larger than the trunks of most trees.

Slightly north, the **California Tunnel Tree** was tunneled in 1895 so that stagecoaches could drive through. In the early 1900s it was used as a "substitute" for the more famous Wawona Tunnel Tree, located in the upper portion of the Mariposa Grove, which was frequently inaccessible due to winter storms. Today you can walk through the California Tunnel Tree. The Wawona Tunnel Tree collapsed in 1969 at the ripe age of 2,200 years. Most likely it died prematurely; the 26-foot-long (8-m), 10-foot-high (3-m) tunnel carved into its base weakened its ability to withstand that year's heavy winter snowfall.

Upper Grove

From the Grizzly Giant, you can continue uphill on the Mariposa Grove Trail to the upper grove, which

the Bachelor and Three Graces, Mariposa Grove

contains the historic **Mariposa Grove cabin,** which sits on the spot where Galen Clark, the first official guardian of Yosemite, once had his home. Nearby is an unusual sequoia known as the **Telescope Tree,** whose hollowed-out trunk creates a telescoping effect if you stand inside it and look upward. It's a 2.1-mile (3.2-km) one-way hike from the shuttle stop to the cabin, and another 1.4 miles (2.3 km) to Wawona Point, an overlook at 6,800 feet (2,075 m) in elevation with a broad view over southern Yosemite. Plan on four hours for the 7-mile (11.3-km) round-trip.

SCENIC DRIVES

WAWONA TO GLACIER POINT

DRIVING DISTANCE: 29 miles (46.7 km) one-way
DRIVING TIME: 1 hour one-way
SEASON: early June to mid-October
START: Wawona
END: Glacier Point

From Wawona, it is a 13-mile (21-km) drive north on Highway 41/Wawona Road to **Chinquapin junction.** With a right turn at Chinquapin (restrooms available), it's 16 miles (26 km) east on **Glacier Point Road** through some lovely forested terrain to **Washburn Point** and Glacier Point. Visit the scenic **Glacier Point overlook** (snacks

Glacier Point Road

and restrooms available). For short hikes to spectacular views, stop at the **Taft Point/Sentinel Dome trailhead** (13.2 mi/21.3 km east of Chinquapin junction) before or after reaching Glacier Point.

BEST HIKES

MCGURK MEADOW AND DEWEY POINT

DISTANCE: 2-7 miles (3.2-11.3 km) round-trip
DURATION: 1-4 hours
ELEVATION GAIN: 300-500 feet (90-150 m)
EFFORT: Easy to moderate
TRAILHEAD: McGurk Meadow
DIRECTIONS: From Highway 41, turn east on Glacier Point Road and drive 7.5 miles (12.1 km) to the McGurk Meadow Trailhead on the left. Park in the pullout about 225 feet (70 m) farther up the road.

Some trails seem to capture the essence of Yosemite, and the McGurk Meadow Trail is one of those. The trailhead is the first one you reach as you wind along Glacier Point Road to spectacular Glacier Point. It's worth a stop to take the short walk through a fir-and-pine forest to pristine **McGurk Meadow,** a mile-long (1.6-km) meadow crossed by a footbridge over a small feeder creek. A few hundred feet before the meadow, the trail passes by an old pioneer cabin, still standing in half-decent repair.

You can turn around at the meadow for a short and easy trip, or you can cross the meadow and continue along the trail until it connects to the **Pohono Trail,** which traverses Yosemite Valley's south rim. An ideal destination is **Dewey Point,** a spectacular promontory located just off the Pohono Trail, with an unforgettable view of Yosemite Valley, taking in

El Capitan, Half Dome, Mount Hoffman, Mount Conness, and the Clark Range. That option turns this hike into a 7-mile (11.3-km) round-trip with only 200 feet (60 m) of additional elevation gain.

SENTINEL DOME

DISTANCE: 2.2 miles (3.5 km) round-trip
DURATION: 1 hour
ELEVATION GAIN: 400 feet (120 m)
EFFORT: Easy
TRAILHEAD: Taft Point/Sentinel Dome
DIRECTIONS: From Highway 41, turn east on Glacier Point Road and drive 13.2 miles (21.3 km) to the Taft Point/Sentinel Dome Trailhead on the left.

It's hard to believe you can get so much for so little, but on the Sentinel Dome Trail you can. The granite dome is about 1 mile (1.6 km) west of Glacier Point, and its elevation

hiking Sentinel Dome

GLACIER POINT ROAD TRAILS

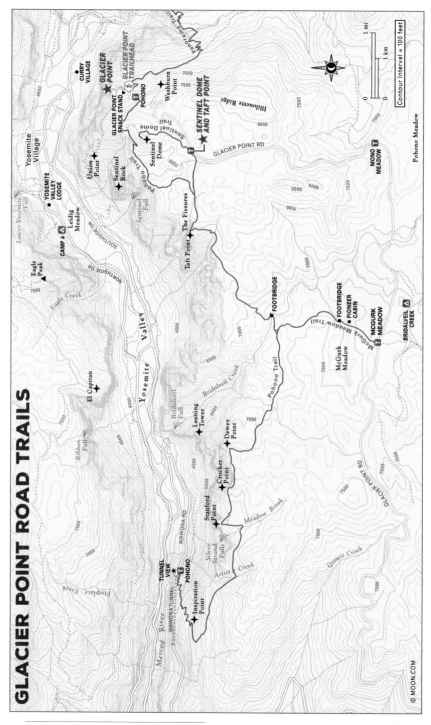

Contour Interval = 100 feet

© MOON.COM

view from Panorama Trail (left); Taft Point (right)

is 1,000 feet (300 m) higher. Views from the dome's summit extend a full 360 degrees. A short and nearly level walk leads you to the base of the dome, and a 300-foot (90-m) climb up its smooth granite backside brings you to its summit. There you are greeted by stunning vistas in all directions, including an unusual perspective on Upper and Lower Yosemite Falls. This is one of the best places in Yosemite to watch the sun set. To make a longer excursion, you can easily combine this hike with the hike to **Taft Point and the Fissures,** which starts from the same trailhead but heads in the opposite direction.

TAFT POINT AND THE FISSURES

DISTANCE: 2.2 miles (3.5 km) round-trip
DURATION: 1 hour
ELEVATION GAIN: 250 feet (75 m)
EFFORT: Easy
TRAILHEAD: Taft Point/Sentinel Dome
DIRECTIONS: From Highway 41, turn east on Glacier Point Road and drive 13.2 miles (21.3 km) to the Taft Point/Sentinel Dome Trailhead on the left.

It's not so much the sweeping vista from Taft Point that you remember, although certainly you could say that the views of El Capitan, Yosemite Valley's north rim, and the Yosemite Valley floor are stunning. What you remember is the incredible sense of awe that you feel, perhaps mixed with a little fear and a lot of respect, as you peer down into the **fissures** in Taft Point's granite—huge cracks in the rock that plunge hundreds of feet down toward the Valley. One of the fissures has a couple of large boulders captured in its jaws; they're stuck there waiting for the next big earthquake or ice age to set them free. After a brief and mostly forested walk, you come out to the metal railing at the edge of **Taft Point's** cliff, where you can hold on tight and peer down at the Valley far, far below. If you have kids with you or anyone who is afraid of heights, be sure to keep a tight hold on them. And don't even consider doing that yoga pose on the cliff edge just to beef up your Instagram account.

POHONO TRAIL

DISTANCE: 13 miles (20.9 km) one-way
DURATION: 6-8 hours
ELEVATION GAIN: 2,800 feet (850 m)

PANORAMA TRAIL

DISTANCE: 8.5 miles (13.7 km) one-way
DURATION: 4-5 hours
ELEVATION GAIN: 3,900 feet (1,200 m)
EFFORT: Moderate to strenuous
TRAILHEAD: Glacier Point
DIRECTIONS: From Highway 41, turn east on Glacier Point Road and drive 15.7 miles (25.2 km) to Glacier Point. Park and walk toward the main viewing area across from the café and gift shop. Look for the Panorama Trail sign about 150 feet (45 m) southeast of the café, on the right.

The Panorama Trail follows a spectacular route from Glacier Point to Yosemite Valley, heading downhill most of the way, but you must have a shuttle car waiting at the end or it's one heck of a long climb back up. A great option is to take the Yosemite Valley Lodge tour bus (209/372-1240) for one leg of the trip.

The aptly named Panorama Trail begins at **Glacier Point,** elevation 7,214 feet (2,199 m). You switchback downhill, accompanied by ever-changing perspectives on Half Dome, Basket Dome, North Dome, Liberty Cap, and, in the distance, Vernal and Nevada Falls. You will gape a lot. After passing **Illilouette Fall** and ascending a bit for the first time on the trip, continue eastward to the Panorama Trail's end near the top of **Nevada Fall.** Turn right to reach the top of the fall and have a rest at the overlook; then continue downhill on the **Mist Trail** on the north side of the river. After a view-filled descent along the north side of Nevada Fall, you'll cross the river in 1.4 miles (2.3 km) and walk alongside lovely Emerald Pool on your way to the top of **Vernal Fall.** Enjoy the show here and then tromp down the granite staircase on the busy trail back to **Happy Isles** in Yosemite Valley.

Note that the route has a 3,200-foot (975-m) elevation loss over its course, but there is also a 760-foot (230-m) climb after you cross Illilouette Creek that is exposed to the sun and often quite warm. Also be forewarned that while the starting miles of the trip are quite tranquil, the final 2 miles (3.2 km) near Vernal Fall can feature a parade of people.

If you're an extremely intrepid hiker, you could hike this trail in the opposite direction (starting at Happy Isles Trailhead and ending at Glacier Point). After savoring the vista from Glacier Point, you can return the way you came for an exhausting 17-mile (27-km) round-trip, or you can loop back to the Valley via the Four Mile Trail. This makes a 13.3-mile (21.4-km) day with a 3,000-foot (915-m) elevation gain on the way up and also on the way down. However, you'll need to have a shuttle car waiting for you at the Four Mile Trailhead or else put an additional 2.3 miles (3.7 km) on your feet as you walk back to your car parked near Happy Isles.

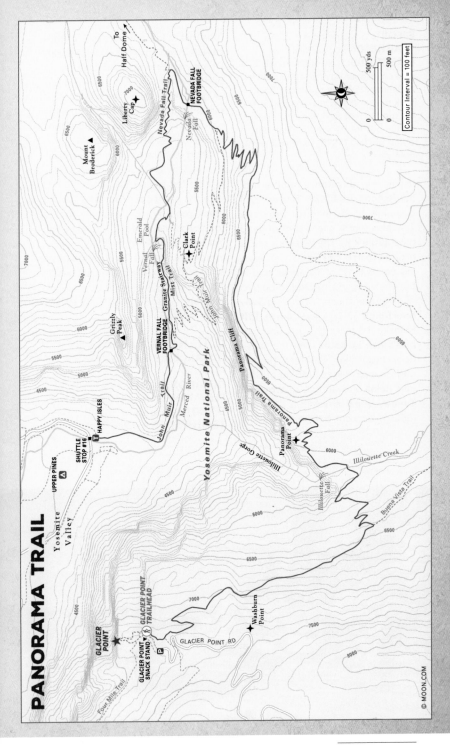

PANORAMA TRAIL

Yosemite Valley

To Half Dome

Liberty Cap

Mount Broderick

Nevada Fall Trail

NEVADA FALL FOOTBRIDGE

Nevada Fall

Clark Point

Mist Trail

Emerald Pool

Vernal Fall

Granite Stairway

VERNAL FALL FOOTBRIDGE

Grizzly Peak

John Muir Trail

John Muir Trail

Panorama Cliff

Merced River

Yosemite National Park

Panorama Trail

Panorama Point

HAPPY ISLES

SHUTTLE STOP #16

UPPER PINES

Illilouette Gorge

Illilouette Fall

Illilouette Creek

Buena Vista Trail

GLACIER POINT

GLACIER POINT SNACK STAND

GLACIER POINT TRAILHEAD

Four Mile Trail

GLACIER POINT RD

Washburn Point

Contour Interval = 100 feet

500 yds

500 m

© MOON.COM

EFFORT: Very strenuous

TRAILHEAD: Glacier Point

DIRECTIONS: From Highway 41, turn east on Glacier Point Road and drive 15.7 miles (25.2 km) to Glacier Point. Park and walk toward the main viewing area across from the café and gift shop. Look for the Pohono Trail sign about 150 feet (45 m) southeast of the café, on the right.

If you can arrange a shuttle trip, the Pohono Trail from Glacier Point downhill to its end at Wawona Tunnel is worth every step of its 13 miles (20.9 km). The two ends of the trail have the best drive-to viewing points in all of Yosemite, and in between you are treated to dozens of other scenic spots, including **Sentinel Dome** at 1.5 miles (2.4 km), **Taft Point** at 3.8 miles (6.1 km), and four bird's-eye **lookouts** over the valley floor: Inspiration, Stanford, Dewey, and Crocker Points. Starting at **Glacier Point** and ending at **Wawona Tunnel,** you'll cover a 2,800-foot (855-m) descent, but there are some

"ups" along the way, too, such as the stretch from Glacier Point to Sentinel Dome, and between Bridalveil Creek and Dewey Point. The trail stays on or near Yosemite Valley's south rim the entire way except for one major detour into the woods to reach the bridge across **Bridalveil Creek.**

Bring along a good map because many of the trail's best offerings are just off the main path. If you don't take the short spur routes to reach them, you'll miss out on some spectacular scenery. Note: The view of **Yosemite Falls** from the Pohono Trail in front of Sentinel Dome is the best in all of Yosemite. For the best overall vista along the trail, it's a toss-up between Glacier Point, Taft Point, and Dewey Point.

CHILNUALNA FALLS

DISTANCE: 8.2 miles (13.2 km) round-trip

DURATION: 4-5 hours

ELEVATION GAIN: 2,400 feet (730 m)

EFFORT: Strenuous

TRAILHEAD: Chilnualna Falls

brink of Chilnualna Falls in winter

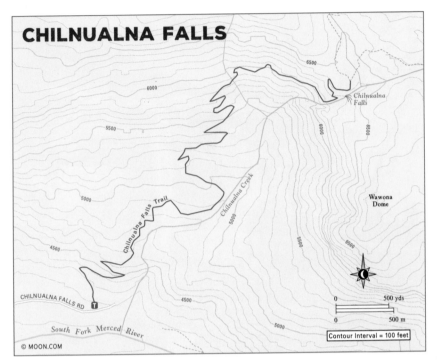

CHILNUALNA FALLS

Chilnualna Falls

Chilnualna Falls Trail

Chilnualna Creek

Wawona Dome

CHILNUALNA FALLS RD

South Fork Merced River

© MOON.COM

0   500 yds
0   500 m

Contour Interval = 100 feet

DIRECTIONS: From the South entrance station, drive 5 miles (8 km) north on Highway 41 to Wawona. Turn east on Chilnualna Falls Road and drive 1.7 miles (2.7 km) to the parking lot on the right side of the road. Walk back to Chilnualna Falls Road and pick up the single-track trail across the pavement.

Are you ready to climb? It's good to be mentally prepared for this hike, which includes a steady, moderately graded, 4-mile-long (6.4-km) ascent, gaining 2,400 feet (730 m) to reach the top of Chilnualna Falls. Pick a nice cool day because this trail is in a lower-elevation region of Yosemite. Your nose will continually pick up the intoxicating smell of bear clover, which joins manzanita and oaks as the majority of the vegetation along the route. The cool spray of **Lower Chilnualna Fall** welcomes you just 10 minutes up the trail; you might want to stick your head in the water before trudging your way up the long series of switchbacks. Halfway up, you get a great view of **Wawona Dome** (elevation 6,897 ft/2,102 m) from a granite overlook. This is a great place to take a break and stretch your hamstrings. Shortly thereafter you glimpse a section of Chilnualna Falls high up on a cliff wall, still far ahead. The path leads above the brink of the fall's lower drop to a series of higher cascades. Keep hiking until you reach the **uppermost cascade,** which consists of five pool-and-drop tiers just 300 feet (90 m) off the granite-lined trail. You'll want to spread out a picnic here before you begin the long descent back to the trailhead.

backpacking the Panorama Trail

BACKPACKING

Some of the best, and least crowded, backpacking opportunities in Yosemite are found in the southern portion of the park. You must have a permit to spend the night in Yosemite's wilderness, and your best bet for information about **backpacking permits** is www.nps.gov/yose/planyourvisit/wildpermits.htm. Backpackers must also take precautions against bears. Hanging food from a tree is ineffective in Yosemite (the bears have long since smartened up to that routine), so use hard plastic bear canisters to store your food for overnight trips.

If you'd rather have someone else plan and guide a backpacking trip for you, contact the experts at **Southern Yosemite Mountain Guides** (800/231-4575; www.symg.com) in Oakhurst.

GLACIER POINT ROAD

From Glacier Point Road, backpackers head to **Ostrander Lake,** or beyond it to Hart Lake. The **McGurk Meadow Trail** leads day hikers and backpackers to the meadow and beyond to Dewey Point (4.1 mi/6.6 km); backpackers can set up camp near **Bridalveil Creek** on the Valley's south rim. Longer trips from Glacier Point Road's **Mono Meadow Trailhead** include Merced Pass (12.1 mi/19.5 km) and around the Buena Vista Crest, or to the Ottoway Lakes (16 mi/26 km), through the peaks of the Clark Range, and then north to Washburn Lake and Merced Lake.

A very popular trail for both day hikers and backpackers is the **Panorama Trail** from Glacier Point. While day hikers follow this trail to drop down to the Valley, backpackers can use it as a route to Half Dome or the Merced Lake High Sierra Camp.

WAWONA

From Wawona, backpackers can head up above Chilnualna Falls to **Buena Vista Peak** (14.4 mi/23.2 km). A popular 40-mile (64-km), five-day loop visits a series of high mountain lakes: Crescent, Johnson, Royal Arch, Buena Vista, and Chilnualna.

BIKING

Bicycles are available for rent in Yosemite Valley, or you can bring your own.

FOUR MILE FIRE ROAD/WAWONA MEADOW LOOP
4 miles (6.4 km) one-way
One option for mountain bikers is to ride the Four Mile Fire Road (also signed as "Wawona Meadow Loop") that begins across from the Wawona Hotel. This old dirt road is one of the few trails in the park where bikes are allowed, although it is much more of a road than a trail—it's a section of an old stagecoach route. The scenery is pleasant, and the gentle grade will give you a chance to spin your wheels.

GLACIER POINT ROAD
32 miles (52 km) round-trip
The challenge of riding Glacier Point Road calls to many a road cyclist.

Despite the fact that the road has a narrow-to-nonexistent shoulder and plenty of vehicle traffic, cyclists pedal this road almost every summer day. If you leave your car at Chinquapin junction and ride out and back to Glacier Point, you'll have a 32-mile (52-km) round-trip with a 2,300-foot (700-m) elevation gain. The toughest part of the trip is the initial 2-mile (3.2-km) climb on the return trip from Glacier Point. Fortunately, you can fuel up with water and snacks at the Glacier Point Snack Stand (summer only) before you ride out. If possible, plan this ride for a weekday, and the earlier in the day the better: The fewer cars you see on this narrow, steep road, the more you'll be able to enjoy the world-class scenery.

SWIMMING

SWINGING BRIDGE
1 mile (1.6 km) from Chilnualna Falls parking lot
The **South Fork Merced River** in and around Wawona is rife with swimming holes and sandy beaches. Many swimmers jump in the river just upstream from the Pioneer Yosemite History Center and its covered bridge, but an even better choice is the big, boulder-lined pool near Wawona's Swinging Bridge. Getting there requires a walk of about 1 mile (1.6 km) up the dirt road from the Chilnualna Falls parking lot, or a 0.5-mile (0.8-km) walk from the end of either Chilnualna Falls Road or Forest Drive.

HORSEBACK RIDING

WAWONA STABLES
209/375-6502; 7am-5pm daily late May-late Sept.
There's no better way to get into the spirit of the Old West than to climb on a horse and ride off into the sunset. Wawona offers horse and mule rides, although you'll have to leave earlier in the day, not at sunset. Two-hour rides depart daily ($85); riders and horses travel the historic wagon road over Chowchilla Mountain and around the Wawona Meadow and golf course into Wawona. An all-day ride to the Mariposa Grove of Giant Sequoias can also be arranged ($150), as well as multiday pack trips into the wilderness. Reservations are strongly advised. Saddlebags are provided for longer rides so you can store a picnic lunch, water, camera, and a jacket. Children must be at least 7 years old and 52 inches (132 cm) tall. Helmets are required for all riders and are available free of charge. The maximum a rider may weigh is 225 pounds (102 kg). The stables are in Wawona, next door to the Pioneer Yosemite History Center.

Swinging Bridge (left); snowshoe trek to Dewey Point (right)

WINTER SPORTS

SNOWSHOEING

The busiest of Glacier Point's snowshoe routes is to **Dewey Point** via the Meadow Ski Trail (7 mi/11.2 km round-trip, 4 hours). Although skiers use this route as well, the vast majority of visitors are snowshoers, many of whom are trying out their functional snow footwear for the first time. The well-marked route is mostly level, with one good climb on the way out to Dewey Point. You can return the way you came or loop back on the Ridge Ski Trail. If the weather is nice, hang out at Dewey Point for a while to enjoy its spectacular view of El Capitan, Half Dome, Mount Hoffman, Mount Conness, and the Clark Range. (Bring a rubber mat or something to sit on, and plenty of snacks and drinks.)

Tours and Guided Walks

Guided snowshoe "adventure hikes" (9am Sun., Wed., and Fri.; $95 includes snowshoe rental; must be over age 13) to Dewey Point are offered in winter. Groups are limited to 7 people. Also offered is an easier "moderate discovery snowshoe hike" (9am and 1pm Mon.-Tues., Thurs., and Sun.; $60 includes snowshoe rental; must be over age 9). To sign up for either snowshoe hiking tour, book online at www.travelyosemite. com or call the Badger Pass Nordic Center (209/372-4996).

SKIING AND SNOWBOARDING
Badger Pass

Glacier Point Road, 5 miles (8.1 km) from Wawona Road turnoff and 10 miles (16.1 km) south of Glacier Point; 209/372-8430 or 209/372-8444 for ski conditions; www.travelyosemite. com; 9am-4pm daily Dec.-Mar.; adult lift ticket $72 all-day, $64 half-day

The only destination you can drive to on Glacier Point Road in winter, Badger Pass offers skiing, snowboarding, and snow tubing, a low-tech version of sledding in which snow lovers slide down the slope on inner tubes ($25 for 2 hours). Lesson packages and equipment rentals are available—just wear your warmest

GLACIER POINT AND WAWONA FOOD

NAME	LOCATION	TYPE
Badger Pass	Glacier Point Road	sit-down
Glacier Point Snack Stand	Glacier Point	takeout
★ Wawona Hotel Dining Room	Wawona	sit-down

clothes, carry chains in your car (or better yet, ride the free shuttle bus from Yosemite Valley), and show up at the ski resort. Sadly, the snowy season in Yosemite is too brief; the resort typically opens in late December and closes on the last day of March.

Today, Badger Pass has five lifts that service 85 acres (34 ha) of ski slopes. With only 10 total runs that are mostly rated as beginner and intermediate, black-diamond lovers won't find much to hold their interest. But for beginners and families, the resort is a great place to spend the day in the snow at reasonable prices.

Free shuttles travel daily from various points in Yosemite Valley to Badger Pass, so you don't have to worry about driving your car in the snow.

FOOD

Aside from the grocery store in Wawona, there are only a few places to find food in the southern area of the park, and two are only open in summer (Glacier Point Snack Stand and Wawona Golf Shop).

STANDOUTS
Wawona Hotel Dining Room
209/375-6556 or 888/413-8869; www.travelyosemite.com; 7am-10am, 11am-1:30pm, and 5pm-9pm daily summer, hours vary in winter; $18-34
You don't have to stay at the Wawona Hotel to eat here—everybody is welcome. The Wawona Hotel Dining Room is popular and the food is delicious. Typical dinner entrées include salmon, pot roast, burgers, and fried chicken. Soups and salads are also available. Be sure to check out the dining room chandeliers made with giant sequoia cones. The restaurant doesn't take reservations unless you have a party of six people or more. Waiting around for a table is not so bad, however; the hotel lounge is always hopping with live piano music and guests making merry. You don't have to dress up for dinner, although some people do.

FOOD	PRICE	HOURS
burgers and fast food	moderate	9am–4pm daily winter only
sandwiches, snacks, ice cream	budget	10am–5pm daily summer only
classic American	moderate	7am–10am, 11am–1:30pm, and 5pm–9pm daily summer, hours vary in winter

In the summer months, a **barbecue** (5pm–7pm Sat.) is held outside on the lawn, complete with heaping portions of corn on the cob, hamburgers, steak, potato salad, and lots more good old American food. If you ever wanted to try square dancing, this is the time and the place. A live band plays and a caller shouts out instructions.

BEST PICNIC SPOTS

There are no picnic areas on Glacier Point Road, but you can always make your own lunch spot on any available granite boulder in or around **Glacier Point.**

Wawona Picnic Area
off Highway 41, 1 mile (1.6 km) north of Wawona, just south of the turnoff for Wawona Campground
This lovely spot along the gentle South Fork of the Merced River is right off the highway, but the sound of the rolling Merced drowns out the sound of cars. With plenty of picnic tables and grills, this is a great place to hang out by the water for a few hours.

Pioneer Yosemite History Center Picnic Area
off Forest Drive, near the Wawona Store
Located just a few steps from the covered bridge leading to the Pioneer Yosemite History Center, this picnic area has eight tables and grills under a shady canopy of incense-cedars, ponderosa pines, and white firs. Nosh on sandwiches here before or after exploring the History Center's historic building or walking the loop to Wawona's Swinging Bridge.

CAMPING

If you'd like to camp in Wawona or near Glacier Point, you'll need to **reserve in advance.** As of 2023, all campgrounds in Yosemite require advance reservations from April–October. This new system is designed to better manage park resources and help visitors have a better experience in the park.

Bear precautions are in effect at

GLACIER POINT AND WAWONA CAMPGROUNDS

NAME	LOCATION	SEASON
★ **Bridalveil Creek**	Glacier Point Road	July–late Sept.
Wawona Campground	Wawona	year-round

all high-country campgrounds. Use the bear box in your campsite to store any item that has a scent, or even looks like food, and you will be rewarded by having a car with all its windows and doors intact.

Reservations and Tips

Reservations for in-park campgrounds are available at **Recreation. gov** (877/444-6777 or 518/885-3639 from outside the U.S. and Canada; www.recreation.gov) and can be made up to five months in advance. Reservations are available in blocks of one month at a time, up to five months in advance, on the 15th of each month starting at 7am Pacific time. Both the telephone and the online reservation systems are open 7am-7pm daily Pacific time November-February, 7am-9pm daily Pacific time March-October.

STANDOUTS
Bridalveil Creek
Glacier Point Road, 8 miles (12.9 km) east of Highway 41; July-late Sept.; $36
There's only one campground on Glacier Point Road, and that's Bridalveil Creek. If you want to camp close to Glacier Point's great day-hiking

trails or be able to enjoy sunsets from the world-famous overlooks at Glacier Point or Sentinel Dome without facing a long drive afterward, this camp is where you want to be.

Although many of the sites are quite densely packed, there are a few winners on the outside of the loops. If you score one of these outer, private sites, you're in heaven. Bridalveil Creek runs right through the camp, and the meadows alongside it produce wonderful wildflowers in July.

The elevation of the campground is 7,200 feet (2,200 m). Of all the camps in Yosemite, this is the one where you want to bring everything you need. If you forgot the hamburger patties, it's a long drive to the nearest store. There is a snack shop (9am-5pm daily) at Glacier Point in the summer months, but it has a very limited menu.

The camp has drinking water, flush toilets, picnic tables, and fire grills. Two **group sites** for groups of 13-30 people ($75) and three horse camps ($60) are also available. Reservations are required for the group sites (877/444-6777 or 518/885-3639 from outside the U.S. and Canada; www.recreation.gov).

SITES AND AMENITIES	RV LIMIT	PRICE	RESERVATIONS
110 tent and RV sites; drinking water and flush toilets	up to 35 feet (10.7 m)	$36	yes
93 tent and RV sites; drinking water and flush toilets	up to 35 feet (10.7 m)	$36	required Apr.-Sept.

LODGING

The historic Wawona Hotel is in the southern part of the park, near the Mariposa Grove of Giant Sequoias and about an hour south of Yosemite Valley. Two additional lodgings are on private land holdings surrounded by the national park: The Redwoods in Yosemite (cabins) and Yosemite West (cabins, rental houses, and bed-and-breakfasts).

Reservations and Tips
Because the rentals at the Redwoods in Yosemite and at Yosemite West are not on the park's central reservation system, they're generally easier to reserve.

STANDOUTS
Wawona Hotel
8308 Wawona Road; 888/413-8869; www.travelyosemite.com; mid-Mar.-week after Thanksgiving and mid-late Dec.; $145-295
The white-and-green Victorian main building of the Wawona Hotel makes an elegant impression. It has a wide veranda out front and porch chairs scattered about its green lawns.

Considered one of California's oldest mountain hotels (one of its cottages was built in 1876; the main hotel was added three years later), the lodge is a great place to stay if you enjoy historic buildings and don't need the amenities of the Ritz. The hotel has a vintage quality, and it's not just due to the preponderance of brass doorknobs, crown molding, Victorian wallpaper, and steam radiators. The building itself is a National Historic Landmark. The room furnishings include wicker chairs, brass beds, and some antique furniture—even a few claw-foot tubs. The **Wawona Hotel Dining Room** is also dependably good.

The 104 rooms are on the small side but comfortable. Those in the main building are not quite as nice as those in various buildings around the grounds. The **rooms with private baths** cost about $60 more; the remaining **rooms without baths** share communal bath and shower facilities, which are surprisingly comfortable and private.

Most other standard hotel services

GLACIER POINT AND WAWONA LODGING

NAME	LOCATION	SEASON
★ **Wawona Hotel**	Wawona	mid Mar.-late Nov. and mid-late Dec.
The Redwoods in Yosemite	Wawona	year-round
Yosemite West	Chinquapin Junction	year-round

are found at the Wawona Hotel, including a swimming pool and a tennis court. A piano player entertains in the main lobby every evening. A major advantage to staying in the Wawona area is the peace and quiet. You're far from the hustle and bustle of the Valley, which is an hour's drive away. Yet the hotel is very convenient to the many trailheads and the spectacular vista point on Glacier Point Road, a half hour away. The Mariposa Grove of Giant Sequoias and the trailhead for Chilnualna Falls are just minutes away.

Wawona Hotel

OPTIONS	PRICE
hotel rooms, some with private baths	rooms from $145
privately owned homes, from small cabins to 6-bedroom houses	2-person cabin from $250, 3-night minimum stay
rental apartments, condos, and homes with 2-6 bedrooms	rentals from $325 for 4 people

lobby of Wawona Hotel

INFORMATION AND SERVICES

Wawona is the main hub for services in the southern part of Yosemite and includes a visitor center, a post office, and a small general store. There are no services at Glacier Point aside from a snack stand and restrooms.

Entrance Stations

South Entrance

The South entrance station is on Highway 41 and provides access to Wawona and the southern part of Yosemite National Park. From the South entrance station to Glacier Point is 39 winding miles (63 km). Plan on 1 hour and 15 minutes for driving.

Arch Rock Entrance

The Arch Rock entrance on Highway 140 is 31 winding miles (50 km) from Glacier Point. Plan on 1 hour for driving.

Visitor Center

Wawona Visitor Center
at Hill's Studio

209/375-9531; 8:30am-5pm daily May-Nov.

The Wawona Visitor Center at Hill's Studio is the main visitor center for the southern part of Yosemite and is located at the Wawona Hotel. Hill's Studio was where the famous 19th-century landscape painter Thomas Hill once worked. Today the center provides information on interpretive activities and programs in Wawona, Glacier Point, and the Mariposa Grove. Books, maps, and wilderness permits are available.

TRANSPORTATION

Getting There

From Arch Rock Entrance

The Arch Rock entrance on Highway 140 is 31 winding miles (50 km) from **Glacier Point;** plan on 1 hour for driving. From the Arch Rock entrance to **Wawona** is 36 miles (58 km); plan on 1 hour for driving.

From South Entrance

Just inside the South entrance is a parking lot for the **Mariposa Grove of Giant Sequoias.** Visitors must park their cars and ride a free shuttle bus into the grove. To get to **Glacier Point** from the South entrance, continue 3 miles (4.8 km) north on Highway 41 to **Wawona,** then another 15 miles (24 km) to Chinquapin. Turn right here and drive 16 miles (26 km) to Glacier Point.

From Yosemite Valley

The drive from Yosemite Valley to **Glacier Point** is a scenic 30-mile (48-km),

1-hour trip south on Highway 41/Wawona Road and east on Glacier Point Road. To reach **Wawona** from Yosemite Valley, take Highway 41/Wawona Road south for 29 miles (47 km), and the **Mariposa Grove of Giant Sequoias** is another 3 miles (4.8 km) farther south.

From Hetch Hetchy

The drive from Hetch Hetchy to **Glacier Point** is 62 miles (100 km) and will take nearly 2 hours.

Parking

You'll find the large **Mariposa Grove Welcome Center parking lot** just inside the South entrance. **Glacier Point** also has a very large parking lot. Smaller trailheads such as McGurk Meadow, Taft Point, and Sentinel Dome have more limited parking, and spaces can fill up early on peak summer days.

Gas and Charging

Wawona has a gas station (near the Wawona Store), but there is no gas anywhere near Glacier Point. The only charging stations inside the park are in Yosemite Valley. Charging stations are also located a few miles outside the South entrance in Oakhurst.

Shuttles

Mariposa Grove Shuttle

8am-8pm daily Apr. 1-Sept. 7, 8am-5:30pm daily Sept. 8-Nov. 7.; free
From April 1 to November 7, free shuttle buses run from the Mariposa Grove Welcome Center parking lot near the Highway 41 entrance station and also from the Wawona Hotel to the Mariposa Grove. You can't drive your own car to the grove unless you have a disability placard or arrive before or after the shuttles' operating times.

Glacier Point Tour Bus/Hiker Shuttle

888/413-8869; 8:30am and 1:30pm late May-late Oct.; round-trip $57 adults, $37 ages 2-12, free under age 2
A tour bus runs from Yosemite Valley Lodge to Glacier Point. Many people purchase a one-way ticket ($29 adults, $19 ages 2-12) and ride from Yosemite Valley Lodge to Glacier Point, then hike back down to Yosemite Valley on either the Panorama or Four Mile Trails. Reservations are available by phone.

Badger Pass Ski Area Shuttle

When Badger Pass Ski Area is open (typically late Dec.-Mar.), a free shuttle bus runs from Yosemite Valley Lodge to the ski area.

Tenaya Lake

TIOGA PASS AND TUOLUMNE MEADOWS

At 8,600 feet (2,600 m) elevation, Tuolumne Meadows extends for more than 2 miles (3.2 km) along the Tuolumne River, making it the largest subalpine meadow in the Sierra Nevada Mountains. From its tranquil edges, trails lead in all directions—to the alpine lakes set below the spires of Cathedral and Unicorn Peaks, to a series of roaring waterfalls on the Tuolumne River, and to the summits of lofty granite domes with commanding vistas of the high country. Tuolumne Meadows is the centerpiece of a huge High Sierra playground for hikers and backpackers and a welcoming place for less ambitious visitors who simply want to sit at a picnic table and wallow in the scenic beauty.

The regions on either side of the meadow, following the 39-mile (63-km) length of Tioga Road from Crane Flat to Tioga Pass, offer more wonders. Two giant sequoia groves—the Merced and Tuolumne Groves—wait to be explored, as do meadows filled with wildflowers at Crane Flat and White Wolf. The drive-to vista at Olmsted Point provides an unusual view of Half Dome and a peek into the funneled granite walls of Tenaya Canyon. Just beyond the overlook, Tenaya Lake sparkles in the sunshine, dazzling visitors with its beauty. Tioga Road reaches the park's eastern boundary at 9,945-foot (3,031-m) Tioga Pass, the highest-elevation highway pass through the Sierra Nevada.

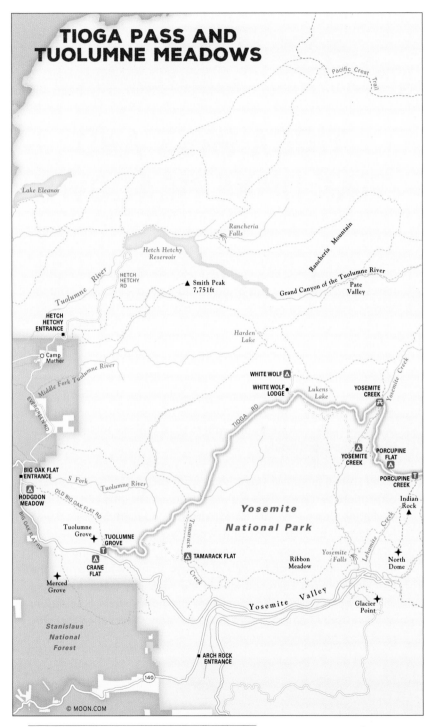

TIOGA PASS AND TUOLUMNE MEADOWS

Lake Eleanor

Pacific Crest Trail

Rancheria Falls

Tuolumne River

Hetch Hetchy Reservoir

HETCH HETCHY RD

Rancheria Mountain

▲ Smith Peak 7,751ft

Grand Canyon of the Tuolumne River

Pate Valley

HETCH HETCHY ENTRANCE ■

○ Camp Mather

Harden Lake

Middle Fork Tuolumne River

EVERGREEN RD

WHITE WOLF 🅰

WHITE WOLF LODGE ●

Lukens Lake

YOSEMITE CREEK 🏕

Yosemite Creek

BIG OAK FLAT ENTRANCE ■

S Fork Tuolumne River

OLD BIG OAK FLAT RD

HODGDON MEADOW 🅰

BIG OAK FLAT RD

YOSEMITE CREEK 🅰

PORCUPINE FLAT 🅰

PORCUPINE CREEK 🇹

Indian Rock ▲

Tuolumne Grove ✦

TUOLUMNE GROVE 🇹

CRANE FLAT 🅰

Yosemite National Park

Tamarack Creek

TAMARACK FLAT 🅰

Ribbon Meadow

Yosemite Falls

Lehumite Creek

North Dome ✦

Merced Grove

Stanislaus National Forest

Yosemite Valley

Glacier Point ✦

ARCH ROCK ENTRANCE ■

(140)

© MOON.COM

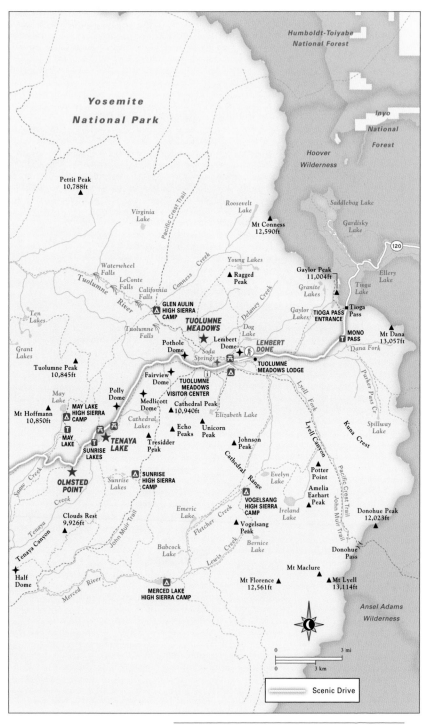

TOP 3

★ **1. OLMSTED POINT:** In a park rife with impressive overlooks, Olmsted Point may be the most impressive of them all. Marvel at the view of Clouds Rest, Tenaya Canyon, and Half Dome, plus dozens of high-country peaks and passes (page 137).

★ **2. TENAYA LAKE:** This deep-blue granite tarn is right alongside Tioga Road, enticing many drive-by sightseers to slam on the brakes and go for an impromptu swim, or picnic along its sandy shores (page 139).

★ **3. TUOLUMNE MEADOWS:** The largest subalpine meadow in the Sierra Nevada, this grassy expanse inspires awe. Numerous trails lead from its edges, but many visitors are happy just to stop for a stroll alongside the Tuolumne River (page 140).

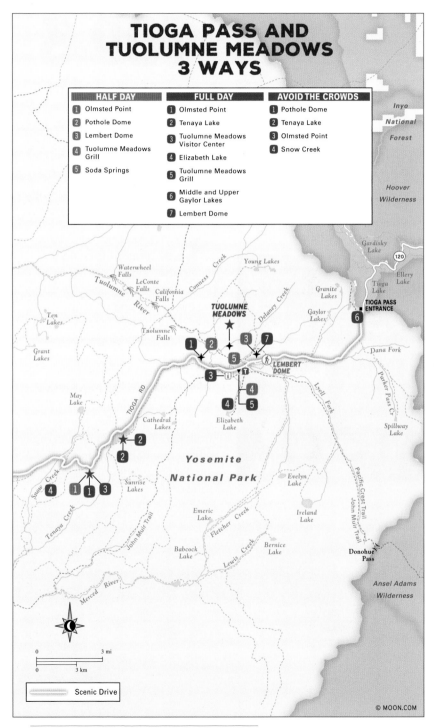

TIOGA PASS AND TUOLUMNE MEADOWS 3 WAYS

HALF DAY
1. Olmsted Point
2. Pothole Dome
3. Lembert Dome
4. Tuolumne Meadows Grill
5. Soda Springs

FULL DAY
1. Olmsted Point
2. Tenaya Lake
3. Tuolumne Meadows Visitor Center
4. Elizabeth Lake
5. Tuolumne Meadows Grill
6. Middle and Upper Gaylor Lakes
7. Lembert Dome

AVOID THE CROWDS
1. Pothole Dome
2. Tenaya Lake
3. Olmsted Point
4. Snow Creek

Scenic Drive

© MOON.COM

TIOGA PASS AND TUOLUMNE MEADOWS 3 WAYS

HALF DAY

This half-day itinerary travels west to east along Tioga Road, but it can also be done in the opposite direction.

1 A drive along Tioga Road must include a stop at **Olmsted Point.** From this overlook, it's easy to pick out the unmistakable profile of Half Dome and the bald ridgeline of Clouds Rest, plus dozens more peaks and precipices.

2 Head east to Tuolumne Meadows' western edge, and take a 15-minute stroll to the top of **Pothole Dome.** An easy walk along the meadow's fringe followed by a gentle ascent on glacially polished granite leads to an inspiring view.

3 Ready for a more vigorous hike? Head to **Lembert Dome's** 9,450-foot (2,880-m) summit for an astonishing view of Tuolumne Meadows and surrounding peaks.

4 Nab lunch (or breakfast, or just a snack) under the big white tent at the **Tuolumne Meadows Grill.** Ice cream cones are big sellers on summer afternoons, but the grill also makes great burgers and breakfasts.

5 Take a stroll over to **Soda Springs** on Tuolumne Meadows' north side. The trail meanders past abundant wildflowers, grasses, and sedges, leading to a permanent spring where carbonated water bubbles up from orange-tinted, iron-rich soil.

FULL DAY

This full-day itinerary travels west to east along Tioga Road, so you can end your day with a beautiful sunset atop Lembert Dome.

1 Stop at **Olmsted Point** and survey the granite landscape chiseled by ancient glaciers and dotted with erratic boulders.

2 Drive 2 miles (3.2 km) east to **Tenaya Lake.** Jump in for a bracing swim or pack along an inflatable raft or inner tube for a mellow float around this cobalt blue lake surrounded by granite domes.

3 Stop in the **Tuolumne Meadows Visitor Center** to learn about the sub-alpine meadow ecosystem and pick up a Junior Ranger packet for the kids. Housed in a historic cabin, the visitor center features exhibits focused on the region's geology, wildflowers, and wildlife.

4 Take the 4.5-mile (7.2-km) round-trip hike to **Elizabeth Lake** from Tuolumne Meadows Campground. Set at the foot of distinctive Unicorn Peak, this gorgeous alpine tarn gives you a taste of Yosemite's high country on an easy-to-moderate hike.

5 You'll be hungry on your return, so head to the **Tuolumne Meadows Grill** to fuel up. Then walk over to a good spot along the Tuolumne River for a quick nap in the sun.

6 Take a two-hour hike to **Middle and Upper Gaylor Lakes,** two startlingly beautiful glacial lakes above 10,000 feet (3,000 m) elevation. Your lungs will definitely notice that altitude.

7 Return to Tuolumne Meadows in time to catch the sunset from **Lembert Dome.** The view from the top of this 9,450-foot (2,880-m) granite dome is awesome at any time of day, but it positively glows at sunset.

AVOID THE CROWDS

This itinerary travels west from Tuolumne Meadows along Tioga Road, but it can easily be done in the opposite direction, starting from the May Lake turnoff.

1 Drive west along Tioga Road, making a quick stop at **Pothole Dome.** There's plenty of space for solitude on top of this broad granite dome, and if you want more subalpine beauty, follow the path beyond the dome to the edge of the Tuolumne River.

2 Walk around to the "back side" (south shore) of **Tenaya Lake,** starting from the beach on the lake's eastern edge. Enjoy the shady pines and gentle sound of water lapping on the banks.

3 Walk the short nature trail at **Olmsted Point.** Get away from the gawking crowds at this astounding roadside vista point by following the short and easy path that leads across the granite to viewpoints of Half Dome, Clouds Rest, and more.

4 Take the May Lake turnoff from Tioga Road, but instead of driving to May Lake's busy trailhead parking lot, park at any pull-off along the access road near **Snow Creek,** where you'll find many quiet pools and cascades for relaxing by the stream.

More Ways to Avoid the Crowds

- Mono Pass (page 150)
- Middle and Upper Gaylor Lakes (page 152)

HIGHLIGHTS

The following sights are arranged west to east along Tioga Road.

MAY LAKE

May Lake Road, 26.6 miles (42.8 km) east of Crane Flat on Tioga Road

May Lake is the site of a popular High Sierra camp located at 9,300 feet (2,850 m). The sparkling waters of May Lake are enchanting—though it is bitterly cold for swimming—and the granite-ringed shoreline is a scenic place to wander and soak up the scenery.

The trail to the lake is easy enough even for young children with an elevation gain of only 500 feet (120 m). It climbs 1.2 miles (1.9 km) to May Lake, tucked in below 10,850-foot (3,307-m) Mount Hoffmann. The trail begins at the **Snow Flat Trailhead** (2 mi/3.2 km off Tioga Road). It passes through a lodgepole pine and fir forest, climbs up a granite-lined slope, and then tops out at May Lake's southern shore. The round-trip walk takes about an hour. Photographers can nab spectacular early-morning shots here, when the calm lake creates a mirror-like reflection of its striking backdrop of granite cliffs.

May Lake is a classic example of a glacial cirque lake, a bowl-shaped basin in which a glacier was formed. Water expands as it freezes, eventually digging out rock to form a large basin, and the resulting basins often fill with water, forming lakes.

From May Lake's western shore, a 2-mile (3.2-km) trail to the summit of **Mount Hoffmann** beckons peak-baggers. The peak is located in almost the exact geographical center of Yosemite National Park, overlooking a vast wilderness panorama that includes Half Dome and Clouds Rest. Adding on this side-trip will add 4 miles (6.4 km) and 1,500 feet (460 m) of elevation change to your day.

★ OLMSTED POINT

shuttle stop 12, about 30 miles (48 km) east of Crane Flat on Tioga Road

Olmsted Point offers a wide-open vista of Yosemite Valley's array of granite domes and cliffs, but from a much different vantage point than anywhere else in the park. First-time visitors may have trouble picking out Half Dome because it looks so different from this angle. Clouds Rest and the skyscraping walls of Tenaya Canyon are also in full view. A 0.25-mile (0.4-km) interpretive trail from this vista point leads through a series of glacial erratics and gives a brief lesson in park geology. Marmots and pikas are often seen poking out from the rocks. If you walk or drive to the far eastern end of the turn-out, you get an interesting look at Tenaya Lake and the multitude of granite domes and peaks beyond it.

view of Half Dome from Olmsted Point at sunset

May Lake

BEST PLACE TO WATCH THE SUNSET

Put on your grippy sneakers and pack along a headlamp or flashlight for an unforgettable sunset at **Lembert Dome.** From the dome's base, it looks impossible to scale, but you can choose from two moderately graded paths to the top—one on the west side of the dome (start at Lembert Dome Picnic Area) and another on the east (start at the Dog Lake parking lot near Tuolumne Lodge). The last stretch to the summit can be a bit intimidating for people unaccustomed to walking on granite, but if you have decent footwear—no flip-flops or slick sandals—you'll be fine. The summit provides unmatched, panoramic views of Tuolumne Meadows and surrounding peaks and domes. As darkness falls, make sure you turn on your headlamp for the steep tromp back down to your car.

Olmsted Point was named for Frederick Law Olmsted, one of Yosemite's first preservationists (and the man who designed New York City's Central Park), and his son, Frederick Law Olmsted Jr., who worked as a planner in Yosemite National Park.

Since most visitors only stop at Olmsted Point for a few minutes, overcrowding is rarely an issue here. At almost any time of day, you'll have a wide choice of parking spots and plenty of room for taking photos.

Look for the Olmsted Point viewpoint on the right side of Tioga Road, approximately 30 miles (48 km) east of Crane Flat.

★ TENAYA LAKE
shuttle stop 9, 32 miles (52 km) east of Crane Flat on Tioga Road

The last of the Ahwahneechee tribespeople were rounded up at Tenaya Lake, ending Native Americans' reign as the caretakers of Yosemite Valley. It's difficult to imagine that sad piece of history on a beautiful August day at Tenaya Lake, when the lakeshore's white sands are lined with picnickers and sunbathers. Plenty of people swim in Tenaya Lake, but the water is chilly. This is a fine place to sit on the beach with a pair of binoculars and watch the rock climbers on **Polly Dome,** just across Tioga Road.

Tenaya Lake attracts a big crowd almost every summer day, but since the lake is so large, you can always find a spot. The lake has two main picnic areas, one on its east end and one near its middle, across from the Murphy Creek Trailhead. Both have picnic tables and charcoal grills. Often many of these tables are empty because the vast majority of Tenaya Lake visitors simply bring their lawn chairs and coolers to Tenaya Lake's beaches, then choose their spots on the inviting white sand. Crowds congregate at the picnic areas and beaches near Tioga Road, but you'll find almost nobody on the lake's southern edge.

Tenaya Lake is 2.5 miles (4 km) east of Olmsted Point.

POTHOLE DOME
shuttle stop 8, 37 miles (60 km) east of Crane Flat on Tioga Road

On the western edge of Tuolumne Meadows lies Pothole Dome, a low granite dome that even young children can hike. An easy, short **trail** parallels the road for about 100 feet

(30 m) to a stand of trees; the dome lies just beyond. Pick any route you like to the top. In less than 15 minutes, you can be on top of Pothole Dome, gazing at the fine view of Lembert Dome, Mount Dana, Mount Gibbs, and, of course, Tuolumne Meadows and its namesake river.

The parking pullout for Pothole Dome is on the north side of Tioga Road, about 5 miles (8.1 km) east of Tenaya Lake and 2.2 miles (3.5 km) west of Tuolumne Meadows.

★ TUOLUMNE MEADOWS

shuttle stop 6, 39 miles (63 km) east of Crane Flat on Tioga Road

Situated at 8,600 feet (2,600 m) above sea level, Tuolumne Meadows is the largest subalpine meadow in the Sierra Nevada, extending for more than 2 miles (3.2 km). The meandering **Tuolumne River** cuts a swath through its grassy expanse. Perhaps more impressive than the wide meadow itself are the majestic granite domes and peaks that surround it. Although the meadow is so beautiful that it is tempting to wander into it, be sure to stay on designated paths. High-elevation meadows are extremely fragile and can be damaged by foot traffic. You can park in several different spots to explore the meadows: In the pullout near **Pothole Dome** on the meadows' west end, at the **Tuolumne Meadows Visitor Center,** or at the **Lembert Dome Trailhead.** Trails lead from all three locations.

Tuolumne Meadows is about an hour's drive east of Crane Flat. Parking and restrooms are available at the Tuolumne Meadows Visitor Center (9am-6pm daily summer) across from the meadow.

Tenaya Lake (top); Tuolumne Meadows (middle); Lembert Dome (bottom)

LEMBERT DOME

shuttle stop 4, 40.5 miles (65 km) east of Crane Flat on Tioga Road

This glacially polished rock is an example of a roche moutonnée, a dome that has one gently sloping side and one side that drops in a steep escarpment. Lembert Dome was named for Jean Baptiste Lembert, a homesteader who lived in Tuolumne Meadows in the mid-1880s. Lembert was something of a hermit who made his living by herding sheep and collecting insects to sell to museums. Rock climbers ply their craft on the highway side of Lembert Dome, but hikers can head around to the back side and walk right up to the summit.

The Lembert Dome Trailhead and Picnic Area (shuttle stop 4) is 1.5 miles (2.4 km) east of the Tuolumne Meadows Visitor Center; a parking lot, picnic area, and restrooms are on the left. You can also access Lembert Dome by hiking from the Dog Lake parking lot near Tuolumne Lodge (shuttle stop 2).

SODA SPRINGS/ PARSONS LODGE

Visitors who want a close-up look at Tuolumne Meadows should take the short walk to Soda Springs and Parsons Lodge on the north side of the meadow. The trail will give you a good look at the meadow

Soda Springs

wildflowers, grasses, and sedges, plus a glimpse into the area's history. Soda Springs is a permanent spring that produces true carbonated water, and it's the site where John Muir and Robert Underwood Johnson discussed the idea of creating Yosemite National Park. The Sierra Club built **Parsons Memorial Lodge** here in 1915, after purchasing this beautiful stretch of meadow so that it could never be developed; eventually the Sierra Club donated the land to the National Park Service.

The **trailhead** for Soda Springs and Parsons Lodge is at a large parking lot off Tioga Road, 0.5 mile (0.8 km) east of the Visitor Center/ Cathedral Lakes parking lot. The lot is signed for Parsons Lodge.

SCENIC DRIVES

TIOGA ROAD

DRIVING DISTANCE: 46.5 miles (75 km) one-way
DRIVING TIME: 1.5 hours one-way
SEASON: open June-September
START: Crane Flat
END: Tioga Pass entrance

Tioga Road (Hwy. 120) is a remarkably scenic drive through red fir and lodgepole pine forest, past meadows, lakes, and granite domes and spires. At its west end, the road starts

at **Crane Flat,** where you'll find a gas station and small store for supplies.

From this 6,000-foot (1,800-m) elevation, Tioga Road slowly climbs its way east through dense forests to the **White Wolf** turnoff at 14 miles (22.5 km). (A restaurant, small store, campground, and restrooms are available at White Wolf.) In another 15 miles (24 km), you reach the pullout for the spectacular vista at **Olmsted Point; Tenaya Lake** is 2.5 miles (4 km) beyond. You have now left the thick stands of trees behind and entered a granite wonderland.

At world-famous **Tuolumne Meadows,** 7.5 miles (12.1 km) beyond Tenaya Lake, you have another chance for snacks and supplies, as well as myriad chances to admire the scenery; then it's on to 9,945-foot (3,031-m) **Tioga Pass,** 7.5 miles (12.1 km) farther. This is the highest mountain pass you can drive through in California. Beyond Tioga Pass, the road exits Yosemite National Park and drops down to Mono Lake, the Eastern Sierra, and U.S. 395.

BEST HIKES

- -

TUOLUMNE GROVE
DISTANCE: 2.5 miles (4 km) round-trip
DURATION: 1.5 hours
ELEVATION GAIN: 550 feet (170 m)
EFFORT: Easy
TRAILHEAD: Tuolumne Grove
DIRECTIONS: From the Big Oak Flat entrance station on Highway 120, drive southeast 7.7 miles (12.4 km) to Crane Flat, and then turn left to stay on Highway 120. Drive 0.5 mile (0.8 km) to the Tuolumne Grove parking lot on the left.

The Tuolumne Grove of Giant Sequoias sits along the old Big Oak Flat Road. Until 1993 you could drive this paved road, but now visitors walk or snowshoe in to see the big trees. Only about 25 giants grow in the Tuolumne Grove, but its claim to fame is that it has one of the two remaining **walk-through trees** in Yosemite. This one is called the **Dead Giant**—it's a tall stump that was tunneled in 1878 so that wagons—and later, automobiles—could drive

through. Go ahead, walk through it. Nobody can resist.

This is a popular destination, so arrive early in the morning to have the best chance at solitude. Leave your car at the parking lot near Crane Flat and hike downhill into the big trees. It's 1 mile (1.6 km) to the first sequoias. At a small picnic area, a 0.5-mile (0.8-km) trail loops around the forest. Make sure you save some energy for the trip back uphill to the parking lot; the grade ascends 550 feet (170 m).

For a longer hike, the old road continues downhill beyond the grove all the way to Hodgdon Meadow Campground. Some people choose to walk the entire 6-mile (9.7-km) distance and have someone pick them up at Hodgdon Meadow.

NORTH DOME
DISTANCE: 9 miles (14.5 km) round-trip
DURATION: 4-5 hours
ELEVATION GAIN: 1,500 feet (460 m)
EFFORT: Moderate to strenuous

TRAILHEAD: Porcupine Creek
DIRECTIONS: From the Big Oak Flat entrance station on Highway 120, drive southeast 7.7 miles (12.4 km) to Crane Flat, and then turn left to stay on Highway 120. Drive 24.5 miles (39.4 km) to the Porcupine Creek Trailhead on the right, 1 mile (1.6 km) past Porcupine Flat Campground.

There are those who say that climbing Half Dome is a bit of a disappointment, and not just because of the crowds. When you reach the top and check out the commanding view, the panorama of granite is not quite as awesome as you might expect, and that's because you can't see Half Dome—you're standing on it.

That's a dilemma that's easy to fix. If Half Dome is an absolute necessity in your view of Yosemite, climb North Dome instead, which offers a heart-stopping view of that big piece of granite. The route is not for the faint of heart, but when you are way up high looking down at Tenaya Canyon and across at Half Dome and Clouds Rest—well, you'll know why you came. The preferred route to North Dome begins at the Porcupine Creek Trailhead on Tioga Road and has only a 1,500-foot (455-m) gain to the summit. A dirt access road quickly brings you to a proper trail, signed as **Porcupine Creek.** Continue straight at two possible junctions near the 2.5-mile (4-km) mark, heading due south for North Dome. After 3 miles (4.8 km), your views begin to open up, providing fine vistas of North Dome and Half Dome and increasing your anticipation. At the trail junction at 4.5 miles (7.2 km), take the left spur for the final hike to North Dome's summit. Surprise—it's a downhill grade to reach it. The view from the top is sublime. Half Dome, just across the canyon, appears close enough to touch. Clouds Rest is a dramatic sight to the northeast. To the southwest, you can see cars crawling along the Yosemite Valley floor.

Tuolumne Grove

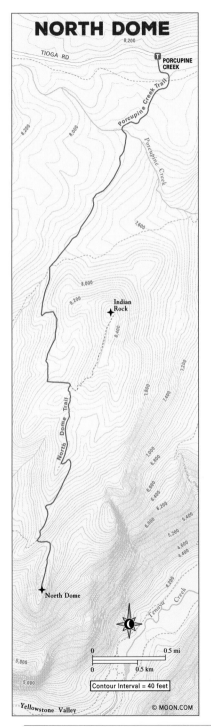

NORTH DOME

TIOGA RD

PORCUPINE CREEK

Porcupine Creek Trail

Porcupine Creek

Indian Rock

North Dome Trail

Tenaya Creek

North Dome

0   0.5 mi

0   0.5 km

Contour Interval = 40 feet

Yellowstone Valley

© MOON.COM

On your return trip, consider taking the spur trail 2 miles (3.2 km) from North Dome, at an obvious saddle. The spur leads a steep 0.25 mile (0.4 km) to **Indian Rock,** the only natural arch on land in Yosemite. It's great fun to climb around on.

CLOUDS REST

DISTANCE: 14 miles (22.5 km) round-trip
DURATION: 7-8 hours
ELEVATION GAIN: 2,300 feet (700 m)
EFFORT: Strenuous
SHUTTLE STOP: 10
TRAILHEAD: Sunrise Lakes
DIRECTIONS: From the Big Oak Flat entrance station on Highway 120, drive southeast 7.7 miles (12.4 km) to Crane Flat, and then turn left to stay on Highway 120. Drive 30.3 miles (48.8 km) to the Sunrise Lakes Trailhead, on the right, just west of Tenaya Lake.

Hiking to Clouds Rest is just as epic as climbing Half Dome, but with far fewer people elbowing you along the way and no permit system to bother with. With a 2,300-foot (700-m) climb and 14 miles (22.5 km) to cover, it's a physically demanding hike. The trail ascends steadily for the first 4 miles (6.4 km), descends steeply for 0.5 mile (0.8 km), and then climbs again more moderately. Keep the faith—the first 2.5 miles (4 km) from the trailhead are the toughest. The final summit ascent is a little dicey because of the terrifying drop-offs; watch your footing on the granite slabs and you'll be fine. Overall, the route is much safer than climbing Half Dome because the final ascent is far more gradual and there are no cables to maneuver. The view from the top of Clouds Rest—of Tenaya Canyon, Half Dome, Yosemite Valley, Tenaya Lake, the Clark Range, and

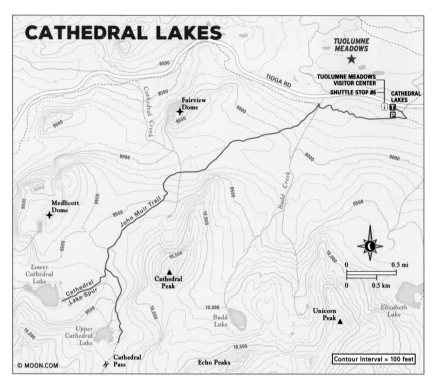

CATHEDRAL LAKES

various peaks and ridges—will knock your socks off.

If this long hike has made you hot and sweaty, you can stop at the **Sunrise Lakes** for a swim on the way back—the first lake is only 0.25 mile (0.4 km) from the Clouds Rest-Sunrise Trail junction.

CATHEDRAL LAKES

DISTANCE: 8.2 miles (12.9 km) round-trip
DURATION: 5-6 hours
ELEVATION GAIN: 1,000 feet (300 m)
EFFORT: Strenuous
SHUTTLE STOP: 6
TRAILHEAD: Cathedral Lakes
DIRECTIONS: From the Big Oak Flat entrance station on Highway 120, drive southeast 7.7 miles (12.4 km) to Crane Flat, and then turn left to stay on Highway 120. Drive 38.5 miles (62 km) to the Cathedral Lakes Trailhead on the right. The trailhead

parking lot is shared with the Tuolumne Meadows Visitor Center; the trail begins on the lot's western edge.

The two Cathedral Lakes make for a tremendously popular, easy backpacking destination in Yosemite, but it's such a short hike to reach them that they also make a great day trip. Located on a 0.5-mile (0.8-km) spur off the John Muir Trail, the lakes are within a classic glacial cirque, tucked below 10,840-foot (3,304-m) **Cathedral Peak.** It's as scenic a spot as you'll find anywhere in Yosemite. From the trail's start near the Tuolumne Meadows Visitor Center, hike 0.5 mile (0.8 km) west to join the **John Muir Trail,** then turn left and head steeply uphill for 3.2 miles (5.2 km), gaining about 1,000 feet (300 meters). Much of the trail is shaded

TOP HIKE
LEMBERT DOME

DISTANCE: 2.8 miles (4.5 km) round-trip
DURATION: 2–3 hours
ELEVATION GAIN: 850 feet (260 m)
EFFORT: Moderate
SHUTTLE STOP: 4
TRAILHEAD: Lembert Dome/Dog Lake
DIRECTIONS: From the Big Oak Flat entrance station on Highway 120, drive southeast 7.7 miles (12.4 km) to Crane Flat, and then turn left to stay on Highway 120. Drive 39 miles (63 km) to the Lembert Dome/Soda Springs/Dog Lake/Glen Aulin Trailhead on the left. The trail begins near the restrooms.

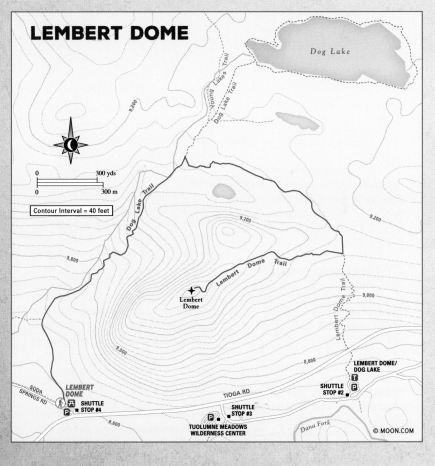

Lembert Dome is a roche moutonnée, which is a French geological term that means it looks something like a sheep. You may not see the resemblance, but you will feel like a mountain goat when you climb to the dome's lofty summit at 9,450 feet (2,880 m). From the parking area at Lembert Dome's base, you may see rock climbers practicing their craft on the steep side of the dome, but the hikers' trail curves around to the more gently sloped back side. You can walk right up the granite—no ropes necessary. The **Dog Lake and Lembert Dome Trail** winds steeply uphill for 0.75 mile (1.2 km) to the dome's north side; turn right and pick any route along the granite that looks manageable. When you reach the dome's summit, you'll be wowed by the view of Tuolumne Meadows and surrounding peaks and domes. You can also hike to Lembert Dome via an eastern trail that starts from the Dog Lake parking lot between Tuolumne Lodge and the Wilderness Permit office. It's at shuttle stop 2.

by lodgepole pines, but when the path breaks out of the trees, views of surrounding peaks, especially distinctive Cathedral Peak, which looks remarkably different from every angle, keep you oohing and aahing the whole way. Turn right on the Cathedral Lake spur to reach the lower, larger lake in 0.5 mile (0.8 km). You'll follow the lake's inlet stream through a gorgeous meadow to the water's edge. Many hikers stop here and go no farther, but it's a pity not to see **Upper Cathedral Lake** as well. To reach the upper lake, retrace your steps to the John Muir Trail and continue another 0.5 mile (0.8 km). Fishing is often better in the upper lake, and the scenery is even more sublime. **Campsites** are found close to the lakes, but you will need to secure your wilderness permit far in advance in order to spend the night.

ELIZABETH LAKE

DISTANCE: 4.8 miles (7.7 km) round-trip
DURATION: 4-5 hours
ELEVATION GAIN: 1,000 feet (300 m)
EFFORT: Moderate
SHUTTLE STOP: 5
TRAILHEAD: Tuolumne Meadows Campground
DIRECTIONS: From the Big Oak Flat entrance station on Highway 120, drive southeast 7.7 miles (12.4 km) to Crane Flat, and then turn left to stay on Highway 120. Drive 39 miles (63 km) to Tuolumne Meadows Campground. Turn right and follow the signs through the main camp to the group camp. The trail begins across from the group camp restrooms near group site B49.

Starting at the trailhead elevation of 8,600 feet (2,600 m), you have a mere 1,000-foot (300-m) elevation gain over 2.4 miles (3.9 km) to get to lovely Elizabeth Lake, set in a basin at

hiking Clouds Rest (top); Cathedral Peak (middle); Elizabeth Lake (bottom)

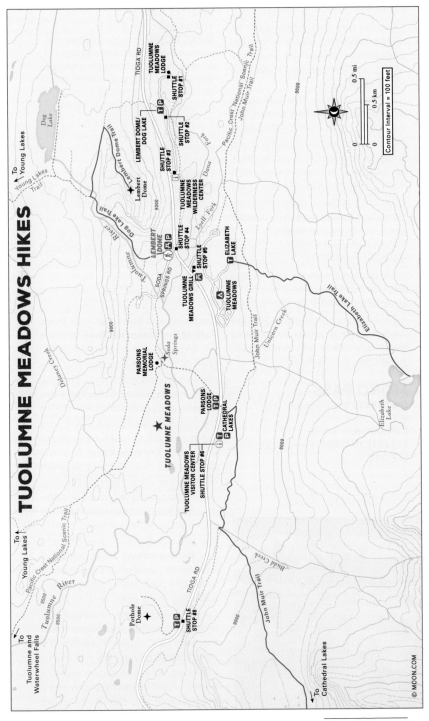

TUOLUMNE MEADOWS HIKES

the foot of distinctive Unicorn Peak. It's a day hike that is attainable for almost anybody, and you can bet that every camper at Tuolumne Meadows Campground makes the trip at some point.

For noncampers, the trailhead is a bit tricky to find—it's tucked into the **B loop** of Tuolumne Meadows Campground, across from the group camp restrooms. Once you locate it, be prepared to climb steeply for 1 mile (1.6 km) and then breathe easier when the trail levels out. Fortunately the route is mostly shaded by a dense grove of lodgepole pines.

On reaching the lakeshore, you'll see that Elizabeth Lake is a gorgeous body of alpine water. Some visitors swim or fish here, and others try to climb Unicorn Peak (10,823 ft/3,299 m), but most are happy to sit near the lake's edge and admire the views of the sculpted peak and its neighbors in the Cathedral Range.

MONO PASS
DISTANCE: 8.4-11.6 miles (13.5-18.7 km) round-trip
DURATION: 5-6 hours
ELEVATION GAIN: 900 feet (275 m)
EFFORT: Moderate

Dana Fork of the Tuolumne River

SHUTTLE STOP: 1
TRAILHEAD: Mono Pass
DIRECTIONS: From the Big Oak Flat entrance station on Highway 120, drive southeast 7.7 miles (12.4 km) to Crane Flat, and then turn left to stay on Highway 120. Drive 44.5 miles (71.6 km) to the Mono Pass Trailhead, on the right, near mile marker T37 (1.3 mi/2.1 km west of the Tioga Pass entrance station).

Thanks to an elevation gain of only 900 feet (275 m) spread over 4.2 miles (6.8 km), you'll hardly even notice you're climbing on the route to Mono Pass. That's if you're acclimated, of course, because you start out at 9,700 feet (2,750 m), where the air is mighty thin.

The **Mono Pass Trail** begins in a mix of lodgepole pines and grassy meadows and then crosses the **Dana Fork of the Tuolumne River,** which is an easy boulder-hop by midsummer. (Earlier in the season you may need to find a log to cross.) The trail soon meets up with **Parker Pass Creek** and parallels it for most of the trip. As you proceed, you'll gain great views of Mount Gibbs, Mount Dana, and the Kuna Crest. At a trail junction at 2 miles (3.2 km), bear left and start to climb more noticeably. When you reach the Mono Pass sign at 3.8 miles (6.1 km), take the right spur trail (unsigned). It leads 0.3 mile (0.5 km) to a cluster of four 19th-century **mining cabins** that have been beautifully restored. It's fascinating to explore the small cabins and surrounding mine ruins and consider the hard life of those who lived and worked here. Then, heading back to the main trail, continue another 0.5 mile (0.8 km) beyond the sign marking Mono Pass for the best views of the trip. From a granite promontory above a tarn, you can see far down

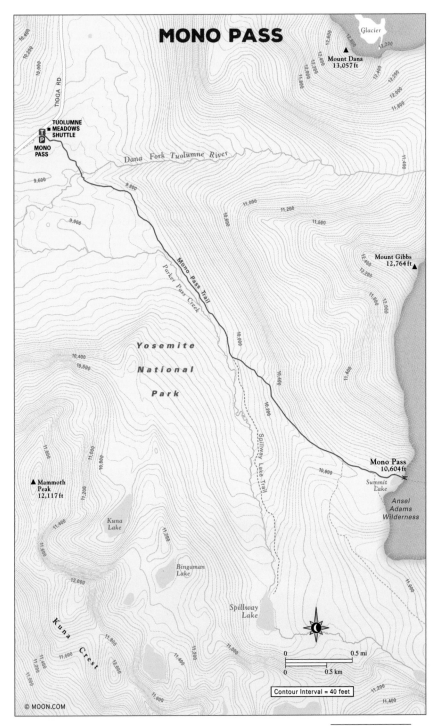

MONO PASS

Glacier

Mount Dana
13,057 ft

TIOGA RD

Dana Fork Tuolumne River

TUOLUMNE
MEADOWS
SHUTTLE

MONO
PASS

Mono Pass Trail

Parker Pass Creek

Mount Gibbs
12,764 ft

Yosemite

National

Park

Spillway Lake Trail

Mono Pass
10,604 ft

Summit
Lake

Ansel
Adams
Wilderness

Mammoth
Peak
12,117 ft

Kuna
Lake

Bingaman
Lake

Spillway
Lake

Kuna Crest

0   0.5 mi

0   0.5 km

Contour Interval = 40 feet

© MOON.COM

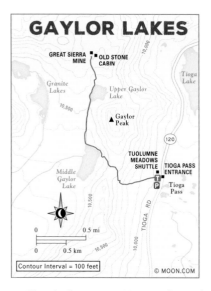

GAYLOR LAKES

GREAT SIERRA MINE
OLD STONE CABIN
Tioga Lake
Granite Lakes
Upper Gaylor Lake
Gaylor Peak
120
TUOLUMNE MEADOWS SHUTTLE
TIOGA PASS ENTRANCE
Middle Gaylor Lake
Tioga Pass
TIOGA RD

0   0.5 mi
0   0.5 km

Contour Interval = 100 feet

© MOON.COM

Parker Pass Creek and its adjoining meadow. Backpackers rarely travel to this lake, so day hikers are likely to enjoy some solitude here. The views of the Kuna Crest and the high alpine meadow surrounding the upper reaches of Parker Pass Creek will take your breath away.

MIDDLE AND UPPER GAYLOR LAKES

DISTANCE: 4 miles (6.4 km) round-trip
DURATION: 2 hours
ELEVATION GAIN: 1,100 feet (335 m)
EFFORT: Moderate
SHUTTLE STOP: 1
TRAILHEAD: Gaylor Lakes/Tioga Pass entrance station
DIRECTIONS: From the Big Oak Flat entrance station on Highway 120, drive southeast 7.7 miles (12.4 km) to Crane Flat, and then turn left to stay on Highway 120. Drive 46 miles (74 km) to the Gaylor Lakes parking lot just west of the Tioga Pass entrance station on the north side of the road.

Middle and Upper Gaylor Lakes

Bloody Canyon to Mono Lake and the surrounding desert.

Another option on the Mono Pass Trail is to take the right fork at 2 miles (3.2 km) and head for **Spillway Lake,** a wide, shallow lake only 1.6 miles (2.6 km) from this junction. You'll have more solitude along this pathway and a pleasant walk alongside

Gaylor Lakes

are deservedly popular destinations because of the short distance required to reach them and their great opportunities for trout fishing. And, of course, there is the draw of the spectacular high-alpine scenery. Starting near **Tioga Pass** (at nearly 10,000 ft/3,000 m), the trail climbs a steep ridge and then drops down to the middle lake. Although it's only 1 mile (1.6 km) of ascent, it's a high-elevation butt-kicker that causes many to beg for mercy.

From **Middle Gaylor Lake,** follow the creek gently uphill to the east for 1 mile (1.6 km) to reach smaller **Upper Gaylor Lake.** Be sure to take the trail around its north side and uphill for a few hundred yards to the site of the **Great Sierra Mine** and the remains of an **old stone cabin.** The Great Sierra Mine turned out to be not so great—no silver ore was ever refined, and the mine was eventually abandoned. The hauntingly beautiful glacial scenery is what remains. Total elevation gain on the hike to Upper Gaylor Lake is about 1,100 feet (335 m), and it's worth every step.

BACKPACKING

Some of the most popular backpacking destinations on Tioga Road, like **Cathedral Lakes,** are also reachable by day hikers, so too many hikers line the trails and crowd the lakeshores, and during the day, you won't have any solitude at your camp. Permits to camp along these popular trails are extremely difficult to come by, especially on weekends. It would be wise to save a trip to high-profile destinations for a weekday in September or early October, when the crowds have thinned.

The following are somewhat lower-profile backpacking trails that lead from Tioga Road or Tuolumne Meadows. On these trails you'll have a greater chance of a true backpacking experience. Remember, though, this is Yosemite: These destinations are still popular, and you can't go without seeing other people.

Also note that if you plan to spend the night in Yosemite's wilderness, you must have a **permit** (209/372-0740; www.nps.gov/yose/planyourvisit/wildpermits.htm). You will also need to take adequate bear precautions;

visitors are required by federal regulations to store all their food properly throughout Yosemite National Park. For backpackers, that means carrying a bear canister.

WATERWHEEL FALLS
16-28 miles (26-45 km)
This hike could be called the Epic Waterfall Trip. If you hike the entire route, you'll see so many waterfalls and so much water along the way that you'll have enough memories to get you through a 10-year drought. To do this trip, you must arrange for a **wilderness permit** in advance or reserve a stay at the **Glen Aulin High Sierra Camp.**

The trail starts near **Lembert Dome** (shuttle stop 4). Begin hiking on the western edge of the parking lot at a gated dirt road signed "Soda Springs .5". You'll follow the Tuolumne River to **Tuolumne Falls** and Glen Aulin Camp, alternating between stretches of stunning flower- and aspen-lined meadows and stark granite slabs. **Waterwheel Falls** is only 3 miles (4.8 km) from the camp,

Ragged Peak frames Lower Young Lake

and two other major cascades, **California Falls** and **LeConte Falls,** are found along the way. Waterwheel is Yosemite's most unusual-looking waterfall. Its churning water dips into deep holes in the granite riverbed and then shoots out with such velocity that it doubles back on itself. When the river level is high, the resemblance to a waterwheel is obvious. The distance to Waterwheel Falls and back is 16 miles (26 km) round-trip.

Beyond Waterwheel Falls you'll have a lot less company. Backpackers who continue onward will keep following the path of the Tuolumne River. The second night of the trip is usually spent at **Pate Valley.** Then with a fresh head of steam you climb up a long series of switchbacks and eventually make your way to Harden Lake and then White Wolf. The trip from Lembert Dome to White Wolf is 28 miles (45 km) one-way. You may be able to get a shuttle bus at White Wolf instead of leaving a car; check with the wilderness office about the current status of the bus system on Tioga Road.

YOUNG LAKES LOOP
12.5 miles (20.1 km) round-trip
Starting from the **Lembert Dome parking lot** (shuttle stop 4), the Young Lakes Loop is a classic Yosemite trip that works equally well as a short backpacking trip or a long day hike. The destination is a series of lakes set in a deep and wide glacial cirque at 9,900 feet (3,000 m) elevation. Because the mileage is short, this is a great trip for a weekend getaway.

The trip starts with a walk down the wide dirt road that leads to Soda Springs—begin hiking on the western edge of the parking lot at a gated dirt road signed "Soda Springs .5". Pick up the trail near Parsons Lodge that leads to Glen Aulin and follow it through lodgepole pines for 1.8 miles (2.9 km) until you see the right turn-off for Young Lakes. Follow the **Young Lakes Trail** for 3 more miles (4.8 km), climbing steadily. At 5 miles (8.1 km) out you'll see the return leg of your loop leading off to the right (signed for Dog Lake).

Continue straight for another 1.5 miles (2.4 km) to **Lower Young Lake,** where you have a stunning view of Mount Conness and **Ragged Peak.** Two more lakes are accessible within 1 mile (1.6 km) to the east. You'll probably want to make **camp** at the lower lakes, but don't miss a hike to the third (uppermost) lake, which is the most visually stunning of them all.

When you're ready to head home, retrace your steps to the junction and take the eastern (left) fork, returning via **Dog Lake** and **Lembert Dome.** Be forewarned: If you loop back this way, it won't be an all-downhill cruise, but the scenery makes the additional climbing worthwhile.

Dog Lake

HIGH SIERRA CAMPS

Among people who love to hike but hate to carry a heavy backpack, the **Yosemite High Sierra Camps** (888/413-8869; www.travelyosemite.com; mid-June–mid-Sept.; $200 adults per night, $100 ages 7-12) are legendary. With nothing on your back but a light day pack with water, snacks, a change of clothes, sheets, and a towel, you can hike through the high country for nearly a week. Along the way, you eat first-rate meals, enjoy hot showers, and sleep on a comfortable cot in a tent cabin each night. The five "camps" are spaced 5.7-10 miles (9.2-16.1 km) apart along a loop trail that begins at Tuolumne Meadows:

- **Glen Aulin** at 7,800 feet (2,400 m) is 5 miles (8.1 km) from the Lembert Dome Trailhead. No showers.
- **May Lake** at 9,300 feet (2,850 m) is 1 mile (1.6 km) from the May Lake Trailhead.
- **Sunrise Camp** at 9,400 feet (2,900 m) is 5 miles (8.1 km) from the Sunrise Trailhead.
- **Vogelsang Camp** at 10,300 feet (3,100 m) is 7 miles (11.3 km) from the Tuolumne Meadows Trailhead. Vogelsang is the smallest and most intimate. No showers.
- **Merced Lake** at 7,200 feet (2,200 m) is 15 miles (24 km) from Tuolumne Meadows or 13 miles (20.9 km) from Yosemite Valley. Merced Lake Camp is the largest with a 60-person occupancy; the others fit 30-40 guests at a time.

The arrangement is basically the same at all five camps, although

ROCK CLIMBING

The preponderance of granite domes in the stretch of highway from Tenaya Lake to the Tuolumne Meadows area makes this region a playground for rock climbers. Two of the best places for watching climbers in action are at **Polly Dome,** directly across the highway from Tenaya Lake, and at **Lembert Dome,** on the east end of Tuolumne Meadows. Two other popular domes for rock climbing in this area are **Fairview Dome** and **Medlicott Dome,** both just off Highway 120 near Tenaya Lake.

YOSEMITE MOUNTAINEERING SCHOOL

209/372-8344; www.travelyosemite.com; classes 8:30am daily June-Sept.; $175-215 per day

The same climbing school that offers classes in the Valley, Yosemite Mountaineering School offers rock-climbing lessons on the granite

each has a different number of tent cabins. Overnight accommodations are "dormitory-style," which means that each tent contains four to six cots; there are a few two-person and eight-person tents. The camp staff tries to keep families and large groups together, but if you are traveling with fewer than four people in your party, you'll probably share a tent with strangers. Breakfast and dinner and are included and are served in a main dining tent; box lunches ($16 adults, $8 children) can be purchased to go. The camps are very social: Meals are served family-style, and the tent cabins are spaced within a few feet of each other, so you'll probably get to know your neighbors.

RESERVATIONS

Reservations are taken on a lottery basis each October, and only a lucky few win. To obtain a spot, submit an **online application** (www.travelyosemite.com) for the following summer during the October lottery. Lottery winners are notified in early winter. Any spaces not filled during the lottery are available for online reservations starting in early March. When summer comes, any remaining open dates (or last-minute cancellations) are listed online (www.travelyosemite.com), so even last-minute planners have a fair chance. Check online availability often to find a spot, or call the concessionaire at 888/413-8869.

GUIDED TRIPS

High Sierra Camp wannabes can sign up for organized five- and seven-day trips led by park naturalists; these cost more but include guide service for your trip. **Guided hikes** ($708 adults for 5 days) and **horseback trips** ($1,320 adults for 4 days) of varying lengths are available. For information on guided trips, phone 209/372-8344.

domes and spires near Tuolumne Meadows. The school conducts seminars and classes for beginning, intermediate, and advanced climbers in the Tioga Road area, and equipment rentals are available. All-day, private guided climbs are also available and start at $360 per person or $175 per person for groups of three people.

WINTER SPORTS

SNOWSHOEING

The trails to the **Merced Grove** and **Tuolumne Grove** (2.5 mi/4 km round-trip) are most often used by snowshoers and sometimes even people wearing regular snow boots, so the snow is usually too chopped up for skiing. Snowshoers will thoroughly enjoy the short treks to the two sequoia groves—it's a special treat to see the big trees crowned with a mantle of snow.

Guided snowshoe **tours** (8:30am-3pm Sat.; $60) to Tuolumne Grove are offered in winter; rates include snowshoe rental and transportation from Yosemite Valley (a shuttle bus departs from Yosemite Valley Lodge). For reservations, call the Badger Pass Nordic Center (209/372-8444) or the Yosemite Valley Lodge Tour Desk (209/372-1240).

Merced Grove
3 miles (4.8 km) round-trip; Merced Grove Trailhead, 3.7 miles (6 km) west of Crane Flat on Big Oak Flat Road
The trail is level and straight for the first 0.5 mile (0.8 km). Bear left at the only junction and head downhill. You will reach the first sequoias, a group of six, at about 1.5 miles (2.4 km). More big trees lie in the next 300 feet (90 m). Only 20 sequoias are found in this grove, the smallest of the three giant sequoia groves in Yosemite, but because they grow very close together, they make a dramatic impression.

CROSS-COUNTRY SKIING
Tioga Road may be closed in winter, but it's still a prime destination for cross-country skiers. The road is plowed up to Crane Flat, usually about 300 feet (90 m) past the parking area for the Tuolumne Grove of Giant Sequoias. The gentle grade of Tioga Road in these first few miles makes great skiing for beginners to intermediates. Highly experienced cross-country skiers head to the **Tuolumne Meadows** region on their skis (since the road is not plowed). Some skiers follow trails from Yosemite Valley to Tuolumne Meadows; others head in from U.S. 395. With a **wilderness permit** (209/372-0740; www.nps.gov/yose/planyourvisit/wildpermits.htm), skiers can camp and ski in and around Tuolumne Meadows for up to two weeks.

Crane Flat (Highway 120 at Big Oak Flat Rd.) is the starting point for several cross-country skiing loops, as well as the popular trek up the snow-covered road to the Crane Flat Fire Lookout Tower (3 mi/4.8 km round-trip).

rock climbing (left); ski tracks on Tioga Road (right)

FOOD

There's nothing quite like high mountain air to work up an appetite. Fortunately, there are a couple of good places on Tioga Road to replenish those calories lost to hiking and recreation.

STANDOUTS
White Wolf Lodge
Tioga Road; 209/372-8416; 7:30am-9:30am and 6pm-8pm daily summer only; $22-29
White Wolf Lodge's restaurant is open to lodge guests and nonguests alike. Dinners might include New York steak, fish of the day, chicken, a vegetarian entrée, and hamburgers. The wine list is more extensive than you'd expect in the high country, and the setting can't be beat, whether you eat inside in the small and cozy dining room or outside on the deck. **Dinner reservations are advised.** A takeout lunch is available noon-2pm daily. Breakfast ($9-13) consists of made-to-order omelets, blueberry pancakes, and fried potatoes. White Wolf Lodge has been in operation since 1927, so they know how to do things right.

Tuolumne Meadows Grill
Tioga Road, shuttle stop 5; 209/372-8426; 8am-5pm daily summer; $7-10
When Tioga Road closes for the winter, seasoned Yosemite visitors dream of the day that Tuolumne Meadows will be free of snow and they can once again eat buckwheat pancakes from the Tuolumne Meadows Grill. This place really knows how to fill up a hiker's empty stomach. The breakfast is highly acclaimed, particularly the biscuit sandwiches filled with egg, bacon, or sausage, and cheese, and the aforementioned buckwheat pancakes. For lunch, the restaurant serves hamburgers, veggie burgers, chicken sandwiches, and surprisingly good salads. The made-fresh-daily vegetarian chili is legendary. Soft-serve ice cream cones are popular on warm summer days. The grill is on Tioga Road across from Tuolumne Meadows, right next to Tuolumne Meadows Store. You can't miss it—and shouldn't.

BEST PICNIC SPOTS
Tuolumne Meadows Grill & Picnic Area
east end of Tuolumne Meadows off Tioga Road
Tuolumne Grill makes the world's best buckwheat pancakes and veggie chili and does a darn good riff on the great American hamburger. Picnic tables are located alongside the Grill and its parking lot, but if you don't want to dine alongside dozens of cars, walk your meal over to the Tuolumne River and find a quiet spot by the water.

Tenaya Lake Picnic Area
park at any of the parking lots near Tenaya Lake
Sparkling blue Tenaya Lake has two main picnic areas, one on its east end and one near its middle, across from the Murphy Creek Trailhead. Both have picnic tables and charcoal grills. Often many of these tables are empty because the vast majority of Tenaya Lake visitors simply bring their lawn chairs and coolers to Tenaya Lake's beaches, then choose their spots on the inviting white sand.

TIOGA PASS AND TUOLUMNE MEADOWS FOOD

NAME	LOCATION	TYPE
★ **White Wolf Lodge**	Tioga Road	sit-down
★ **Tuolumne Meadows Grill**	Tuolumne Meadows (shuttle stop 5)	takeout
Tuolumne Meadows Lodge Dining Room	Tuolumne Meadows (shuttle stop 1)	sit-down

Lembert Dome Picnic Area
on Tioga Road, 0.25 mile (0.4 km) east of Tuolumne Meadows Campground

Clearly visible from Tioga Road at the base of Lembert Dome, this picnic area is a bit too close to the parking lot and its steady stream of cars, but you can't beat the view of Lembert's polished granite. Six picnic tables sit right next to the parking lot, but if you can picnic without a table, walk a few hundred feet around the "foot" of the dome until you find the perfect spot.

Yosemite Creek Picnic Area
on Tioga Road, 19.5 miles (31.4 km) east of Crane Flat, across from the Ten Lakes Trailhead

It's easy to miss this picnic area altogether since it can't be seen from Tioga Road, but it's a lovely spot for some quiet nature time. Follow the winding access road down to Yosemite Creek, where you'll find a half-dozen picnic tables, a vault toilet, and a good chance of solitude alongside the gushing stream, massive pines and firs, and granite boulders.

picnic area at Tenaya Lake (left); Yosemite Creek Picnic Area (right)

FOOD	PRICE	HOURS
classic American	moderate	7:30am-9:30am and 6pm-8pm daily summer only
casual American	budget	8am-5pm daily summer
classic American	moderate	7am-9am and 5:30pm-8pm daily summer

CAMPING

If you'd like to camp in Yosemite's high country along Tioga Road, you'll need to reserve in advance. As of 2023, all campgrounds in Yosemite require advance reservations from April to October. This new system is designed to better manage park resources and help visitors have a better experience in the park.

Bear precautions are in effect at all high-country campgrounds. Use the bear box in your campsite to store any item that has a scent, or even looks like food, and you will be rewarded by having a car with all its windows and doors intact.

RESERVATIONS

Make a camping reservation at **Recreation.gov** (877/444-6777 or 518/885-3639 from outside the U.S. and Canada, www.recreation.gov) up to five months in advance. Reservations are available in blocks of one month at a time, on the 15th of each month starting at 7am Pacific time. Both the telephone and the online reservation systems are open 7am-7pm daily Pacific time

November-February and 7am-9pm daily March-October.

STANDOUTS
White Wolf
late June-mid-Sept.; $30

White Wolf (74 sites) is a favorite of many who come to Yosemite year after year. Reservations are required, and you have a decent chance of getting a site most nights, except Saturday and possibly Friday. Besides its location, White Wolf is popular because it has all the advantages of a fully developed car campground, including flush toilets. An even greater luxury is **White Wolf Lodge** (about 300 ft/90 m from the camp), where you can enjoy delicious homemade meals if you don't feel like blackening another hot dog. The lodge also has a small store that sells drinks and snacks.

The camp has a pleasant setting at 8,000 feet (2,400 m) elevation amid a forest of lodgepole pine. Some sites are tucked in among rocky boulders and others are on the outside of the loop among the

TIOGA PASS AND TUOLUMNE MEADOWS CAMPGROUNDS

NAME	LOCATION	SEASON
Hodgdon Meadow	Highway 120	year-round
Crane Flat	Highway 120	July-mid-Oct.
Tamarack Flat	off Tioga Road	late June-mid-Oct.
★ **White Wolf**	off Tioga Road	late June-mid-Sept.
Yosemite Creek	off Tioga Road	late June-early Sept. weather permitting
Porcupine Flat	Tioga Road	July-mid-Oct.
Tuolumne Meadows	Tuolumne Meadows (shuttle stop 5)	late June-late Sept.

trees, so you can achieve a modicum of privacy. However, the sites are packed in too densely for this small area. Small RVs (less than 27 ft/8 m) can fit in here. The camp has drinking water, flush toilets, picnic tables, and fire grills. Trails to Harden Lake and Lukens Lake lead right from the camp and the lodge, and many other trails are close by.

SITES AND AMENITIES	RV LIMIT	PRICE	RESERVATIONS
105 tent and RV sites; flush toilets and drinking water	up to 35 feet (10.7 m)	$36	required
166 tent and RV sites; flush toilets and drinking water	up to 35 feet (10.7 m)	$36	required
52 tent sites; vault toilets; accessible sites available	RVs not recommended	$24	required
74 tent and RV sites; flush toilets and drinking water; accessible sites available	up to 27 feet (8 m)	$30	required
75 tent sites; vault toilets; accessible sites available	no RVs	$24	required
52 tent and small RV sites; vault toilets; accessible sites available	up to 24 feet (7.3 m)	$20	required
304 tent and RV sites; flush toilets and drinking water; accessible sites available	up to 35 feet (10.7 m)	$36	required

From Crane Flat, drive 14 miles (22.5 km) east on Highway 120. Turn left at the White Wolf sign and drive 1 mile (1.6 km) to the campground. The camp access road is smoothly paved, so it's easy to cruise in and look for a spot. If you strike out, just head for one of the other camps on Tioga Road.

TIOGA PASS AND TUOLUMNE MEADOWS LODGING

NAME	LOCATION	SEASON
★ White Wolf Lodge	Tioga Road	mid-June-early Sept.
Tuolumne Meadows Lodge	Tuolumne Meadows (shuttle stop 1)	mid-June-mid-Sept.

LODGING

Two rustic camp-style lodgings—White Wolf Lodge and Tuolumne Lodge—are located in Yosemite's high country on Tioga Road, but these are open only June-September.

RESERVATIONS

Reservations are made through **Aramark's Yosemite Hospitality** (888/413-8869; www.travelyosemite.com). The reservations phone line is open 7am-8pm Monday-Friday and 7am-7pm Saturday-Sunday (hours may be shorter in winter), or you can reserve online 24 hours daily. It is wise to make reservations far in advance for the busy summer season. Cancellations happen frequently, so if you strike out, keep calling back.

STANDOUTS
White Wolf Lodge
Tioga Road; 888/413-8869; www.travelyosemite.com; mid-June-early Sept.; $137-156

The first time you glimpse the cabins at White Wolf Lodge, you sense the realization of your Yosemite lodging dreams. Set at the sweet high-country elevation of 8,000 feet (2,400 m), the white wooden cabins are trimmed in hunter green, with Adirondack chairs lined up on the porches to face a wildflower-filled meadow. If you think that high-country lodgings don't get much better than this, you're exactly right.

However, only four units are the quaint *Sunset* magazine-style

White Wolf Campground (left); cabin at White Wolf Lodge (right)

OPTIONS	PRICE
tent cabins and wooden cabins	tent cabins from $137; wooden cabins from $156
tent cabins	tent cabins from $137

wooden cabins ($156). These have their own baths, propane heat, daily maid service, a desk, a chair, a dresser, two double beds, and electricity generated only during certain hours of the day.

Right behind the wooden cabins are 24 typical Yosemite **tent cabins**—large off-white tents on raised wooden platforms, almost bare inside except for a wood-burning stove, candles for lighting (there is no electricity), and a couple of beds with linens. The tent cabins are more plentiful and easier to reserve, but they're also bare-bones. You'll walk to a communal bath for toilets and showers. Regardless of which type of cabin you reserve, everything about a stay at White Wolf is easy. An excellent **restaurant** on the premises serves breakfast and dinner and makes box lunches to go. A small store sells snacks, drinks, and a few minimal supplies. A couple of hiking trails begin at your doorstep, and a multitude of trails on Tioga Road are just a few miles away. Yosemite Valley is a one-hour drive.

So how do you get one of those white-and-green cabins? Plan on reserving at least a year in advance.

INFORMATION AND SERVICES

Services are limited in this part of Yosemite. **Tuolumne Meadows,** with its visitor center, store, restaurant, and post office, has the most services along Tioga Road. **Crane Flat,** at the western end of Tioga Road, has a gas station with a well-stocked store.

Entrance Stations
Big Oak Flat Entrance
Highway 120

The Big Oak Flat entrance station on Highway 120 offers western access to Tioga Road and Tuolumne Meadows. This entrance is open year-round, but tire chains may be required in the winter months.

Tioga Pass Entrance
June-Sept.

To the east is the Tioga Pass entrance station, which offers seasonal access through the park and from the Eastern Sierra.

Visitor Centers
Tuolumne Meadows Visitor Center
209/372-0263; 8am-5pm daily summer only

The second-largest of the park's visitor centers is located on the west end of Tuolumne Meadows, on the south side of Tioga Road. Open from Tioga Road's opening date until late September, the Tuolumne Meadows Visitor Center is housed in a historic building that often has a cozy fire burning in the fireplace. Exhibits focus on the area's geology, wildflowers, wildlife, and ecology. A few displays interpret humans' relation to the Yosemite high country, including John Muir's perspective on the value of Yosemite as a national park. Books and maps are for sale.

Big Oak Flat Information Station
8am-5pm daily year-round

For visitors driving into the park through the Big Oak Flat entrance on Highway 120, the small Big Oak Flat Information Station is 100 feet (30 m) south of the entrance kiosk, on the west side of the road. A few books and maps are for sale, and wilderness permits may be available.

TRANSPORTATION
Getting There

Tioga Pass, at the eastern end of the park, is 46.5 miles (75 km) from **Crane Flat** (the starting point of Tioga Road),

about a 1.5-hour drive without stopping.

From Big Oak Flat Entrance

From the Big Oak Flat entrance on Highway 120, drive southeast 7.7 miles (12.4 km) to Crane Flat (the drive takes 10-15 minutes), and then turn left onto Tioga Road/Highway 120.

From Yosemite Valley

To drive to Tioga Pass from Yosemite Valley, plan on about **two hours** from the time you leave the Valley until the time you reach the Tioga Pass entrance station. It will take about 30 minutes (north along Big Oak Flat Road) to get to **Crane Flat** and the start of Tioga Road, which is 20 miles (32 km) north of the main lodgings and campgrounds in Yosemite Valley via Big Oak Flat Road. It's another 1.5 hours to Tioga Pass.

Parking

Most popular sights, trailheads, and picnic areas along Tioga Road have parking lots, including Lembert Dome, Tenaya Lake, Olmsted Point, and the Tuolumne Meadows Visitor Center.

Gas and Charging

There is a gas station at **Crane Flat.**
There are no other gas stations along Tioga Road inside the park. On the eastern end, your first chance for gas will be the **Tioga Gas Mart,** 11 miles (17.7 km) east of Tioga Pass, outside the park. The only charging stations inside the park are in Yosemite Valley, but you can charge your vehicle at **Rush Creek Lodge,** just 1.6 miles (2.6 km) west of Yosemite's Big Oak Flat entrance on Highway 120. A charging station is also available at **Evergreen Lodge** on Hetch Hetchy Road.

Shuttle

Tuolumne Meadows Shuttle

www.travelyosemite.com; 7am-7pm daily June-Sept.; day pass $10 adults, $5 ages 12-18, weekly pass $25 adults, $12.50 ages 12-18

During the summer months, the Tuolumne Meadows Shuttle runs along Tioga Road, stopping at all major trailheads between Olmsted Point and Tioga Pass. The first shuttle of the day leaves Tuolumne Meadows Lodge at 7am; shuttles arrive at each stop at approximately 30-minute intervals. Check online or at the Tuolumne Meadows Visitor Center, White Wolf, or Tuolumne Meadows Lodge for a detailed schedule.

hiking at Hetch Hetchy

HETCH HETCHY

Most everybody in California has visited Yosemite Valley, but substantially fewer people have visited Hetch Hetchy, Yosemite's "twin" in the park's northwest corner. Granite-lined Hetch Hetchy Valley was flooded in 1923 to create a water supply for the growing city of San Francisco. It was the sad end of a long fight for naturalist John Muir, who battled in vain to save Hetch Hetchy from the big-city politicians.

Muir described Hetch Hetchy Valley as Yosemite Valley's "wonderfully exact counterpart." Although smaller in size, Hetch Hetchy was shaped by the same geological forces that created Yosemite's glacially carved valley. Despite the fact that Hetch Hetchy's granite walls now hem in a 306-foot-deep (93-m) reservoir, its similarities to Yosemite are still striking: The pristine granite of Kolana Rock and Hetch Hetchy Dome juts up into the sky, waterfalls drop hundreds of feet from hanging valleys, and flower-filled meadows line the edge of the meandering Tuolumne River.

Even though humans have permanently altered Hetch Hetchy, its beauty prevails. Hike along the reservoir's shoreline and you'll see wildflowers blooming in the understory of massive ponderosa pines and incense-cedars. Birds and other wildlife thrive with the abundance of year-round water. And in spring—the best time to visit—Hetch Hetchy's waterfalls still flow with exuberance.

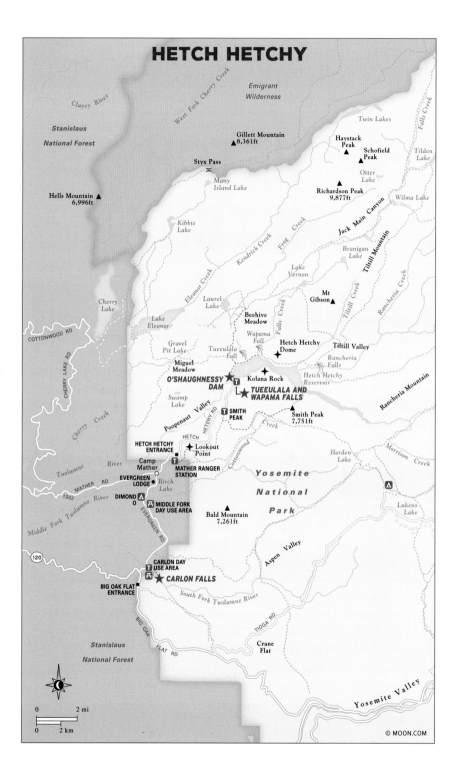

TOP 3

1. O'SHAUGHNESSY DAM: See the remarkable feat of engineering that forms Hetch Hetchy Reservoir. In spring, its overflow valves spray thousands of gallons of water into the free-flowing stretch of the Tuolumne River (page 177).

2. TUEEULALA AND WAPAMA FALLS: In spring and early summer, these two spectacular waterfalls drop more than 1,000 feet (300 m) to the lakeshore at Hetch Hetchy. To see them up close, take a hike along the reservoir's edge and enjoy a fabulous wildflower display (page 179).

3. CARLON FALLS: A favorite swimming hole for more than 100 years, the pools below Carlon Falls make a fine destination for a short hike on a hot summer day. Go all the way to the falls or just stop at any inviting spot along the river (page 182).

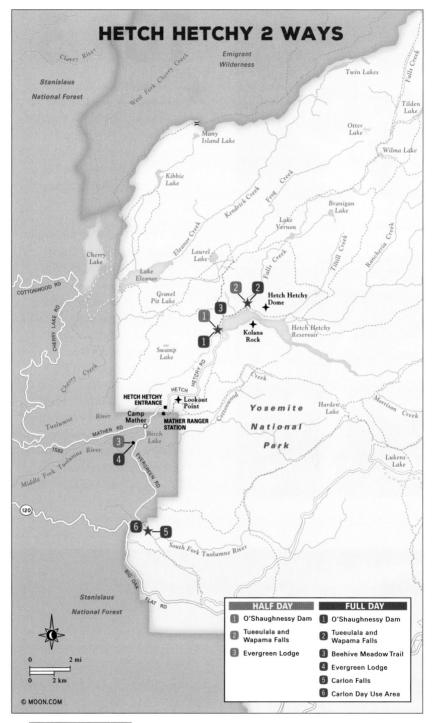

HETCH HETCHY 2 WAYS

Clavey River

Emigrant Wilderness

Twin Lakes

Falls Creek

Stanislaus National Forest

West Fork Cherry Creek

Tilden Lake

Many Island Lake

Otter Lake

Wilma Lake

Kibbie Lake

Kendrick Creek

Frog Creek

Branigan Lake

Lake Vernon

Rancheria Creek

Cherry Lake

Eleanor Creek

Laurel Lake

Falls Creek

Tuitill Creek

COTTONWOOD RD

Lake Eleanor

Gravel Pit Lake

2 2 **Hetch Hetchy Dome**

Hetch Hetchy Reservoir

CHERRY LAKE RD

1 3

1 **Kolana Rock**

Swamp Lake

HETCHY RD

HETCH

Cherry Creek

HETCH HETCHY ENTRANCE ✦ **Lookout Point**

Cottonwood Creek

Yosemite

Harden Lake

Morrison Creek

Camp Mather ○

Tuolumne River

MATHER RD

MATHER RANGER STATION

National

TS02

Birch Lake

3
4

EVERGREEN RD

Park

Middle Fork Tuolumne River

Lukens Lake

120

6 ✦ 5

South Fork Tuolumne River

BIG OAK FLAT RD

Stanislaus National Forest

HALF DAY	FULL DAY
1 O'Shaughnessy Dam	1 O'Shaughnessy Dam
2 Tueeulala and Wapama Falls	2 Tueeulala and Wapama Falls
3 Evergreen Lodge	3 Beehive Meadow Trail
	4 Evergreen Lodge
	5 Carlon Falls
	6 Carlon Day Use Area

N

0 ____ 2 mi
0 ____ 2 km

© MOON.COM

HETCH HETCHY 2 WAYS

HALF DAY

1 Start your Hetch Hetchy exploration with a stroll across **O'Shaughnessy Dam**'s concrete crest, admiring the granite domes, sheer cliffs, and cobalt blue waters of 8-mile-long (12.9-km) Hetch Hetchy Reservoir, plus springtime water-falls tumbling more than 1,000 feet (300 m).

2 On the dam's far side, walk through a 500-foot-long (150-m) tunnel to access the lakeshore trail to **Tueeulala and Wapama Falls,** a tumbling cataract that gushes with snowmelt in the spring months (best Mar.-May). You'll pass rib-bonlike Tueeulala Fall along the way, plus wildflower carpets of purple larkspur, harlequin lupine, and pink farewell-to-spring. Plan on a few hours for this 4.8-mile (7.7-km) round-trip.

3 After the hike, a hearty lunch and a microbrew will hit the spot, so backtrack 9 miles (14.5 km) on Evergreen Road to **Evergreen Lodge.**

FULL DAY

1 Start with a morning walk across **O'Shaughnessy Dam.** Take in the vistas of Kolana Rock, Hetch Hetchy Dome, and the immense blue lake.

2 Walk through the tunnel to access the trail to **Tueeulala and Wapama Falls.**

3 On your return trip from the fall, get a heart-rate spike and a bird's-eye view by climbing the steep switchbacks up **Beehive Meadow Trail,** its edges lined with vivid floral displays.

4 Recharge (you'll need it after that hike) with a break and lunch at **Evergreen Lodge.**

5 Get ready for another hike, this one combined with a refreshing swim. Drive north on Evergreen Road to the Carlon Falls Trailhead. Walk 2.2 miles (3.5 km) alongside the mellow South Fork of the Tuolumne River to **Carlon Falls,** a glistening cataract with a dependable year-round flow. Enjoy a cool dip in the falls' pool.

6 After the hike, walk across the bridge from the Carlon Falls trailhead to **Carlon Day Use Area** for a breather. The Tuolumne River is so clear, you can easily spot fish swimming above the rocky riverbed.

AVOID THE CROWDS

Hetch Hetchy is nearly always an oasis of calm within busy Yosemite National Park. You won't find crowds here except for peak weekends in springtime, when the reservoir's waterfalls flow furiously and wildflowers burst into bloom. If you happen to visit on a busy day, get away from the crowds by taking the short hike to **Lookout Point** for a long-distance view of Hetch Hetchy. Or if you're up for an adventure, tackle the 13-mile (21-km) round-trip to 7,751-foot (2,363-m) **Smith Peak,** this region's highest summit.

view from Smith Peak

Since the Hetch Hetchy Road closes at sunset every evening, you can't watch a sunset-color show inside the Hetch Hetchy gates. But if you park outside the gates near the Mather Ranger Station, you can take the short hike to **Lookout Point** to catch a 360-degree sunset (don't forget a flashlight for the return trip in the dark). From the bald granite knob of Lookout Point, you can glimpse Hetch Hetchy Reservoir and its springtime waterfalls, plus a wide-angle view of the Tuolumne River Canyon.

HIGHLIGHTS

★ O'SHAUGHNESSY DAM

7.5 miles (12.1 km) north of Hetch Hetchy entrance on Hetch Hetchy Road; 7am-9pm daily May-Labor Day, shorter hours in winter, may be closed for brief periods during winter storms

Built by the City of San Francisco between 1914 and 1923 to provide power and water for its citizens, O'Shaughnessy Dam was a product of its time. Although the dam's construction was adamantly opposed by John Muir, the Sierra Club, the Pacific Gas and Electric Company, and the cities of Turlock and Modesto—all for their own reasons—the dam came into existence because of a piece of Congressional legislation called the Raker Act, signed into law by President Woodrow Wilson.

The prevailing political mood at the time, particularly at the federal level, could not allow the preservation of a national park to be more important than the twin themes of progress and development. And so the massive dam was built, Hetch Hetchy Valley was flooded, and the world will never again see the twin to Yosemite Valley in its pristine state.

Whatever else we may think or say about it, the dam is a remarkable feat of engineering. It took almost 7 years to build, and another 14 years before the aqueduct lines were completed over the 155-mile (250-km) course to San Francisco, which required building 37 miles (60 km) of tunnels. The system operates entirely by gravity. The original cost of construction was more than $12 million—a fortune at the time. When the reservoir's water finally flowed to San Francisco, the cost had risen to $100 million. But the building didn't stop. In 1938, the original dam was modified, raising its height by 85 feet (26 m). Currently, the dam can hold back approximately 117 billion gallons (445 million cubic meters) of water.

The **Hetch Hetchy Reservoir** is 8 miles (12.9 km) long and 306 feet (93 m) deep at its deepest point. No swimming is allowed in the water supply. After parking at the dam, be sure to walk across its massive 600-foot-long (185-m) concrete surface. If this is your first trip to this part of Yosemite, be sure to stop and read the interpretive plaques that explain the building of Hetch Hetchy Reservoir and its service to San Francisco.

BEST HIKES

LOOKOUT POINT

DISTANCE: 2.8 miles (4.5 km) round-trip
DURATION: 1.5 hours
ELEVATION GAIN: 600 feet (185 m)
EFFORT: Easy
TRAILHEAD: Mather Ranger Station
DIRECTIONS: Drive north on Evergreen Road (1 mi/1.6 km west of the Big Oak Flat entrance to Yosemite) for 7.4 miles (11.9 km) and turn right onto Hetch Hetchy Road. Drive 1.5 miles (2.4 km) to the Hetch Hetchy entrance station; the trail begins 300 feet (90 m) past the kiosk, just beyond the ranger station on the right.

Check your calendar. Is it springtime? Are most of the high-country trails in Yosemite National Park still snowed in? Then it's time to take the easy jaunt to Lookout Point, where you can admire Hetch Hetchy Reservoir

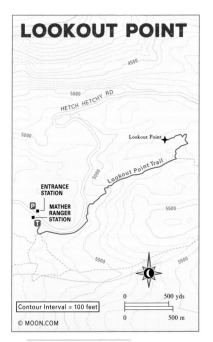

LOOKOUT POINT

4500

5000

HETCH HETCHY RD

5000

Lookout Point

5000

Lookout Point Trail

ENTRANCE STATION

P MATHER RANGER STATION

5500

5000

5500

Contour Interval = 100 feet

0   500 yds

0   500 m

© MOON.COM

and its waterfalls from an unusual perspective and count the plentiful wildflowers along the trail as you walk. The Lookout Point Trail begins near the Mather Ranger Station on Hetch Hetchy Road. Begin hiking at the trail sign for **Cottonwood** and **Smith Meadows.** Turn left at the first **junction;** then follow the trail as it roughly parallels Hetch Hetchy Road for 0.5 mile (0.8 km). The trail turns away from the road with a brief uphill stretch and then enters a level, forested area that was severely burned in the wildfires of 1996. This is where the flowers bloom profusely in springtime.

Look for a trail junction at 1 mile (1.6 km) out, and bear left for Lookout Point, 0.3 mile (0.5 km) away. The path gets rather faint in places, but **rock cairns** mark the way. Just head for the highest point you see atop a granite knob dotted with a few pines. You'll know you're at Lookout Point when you can see the west end of Hetch Hetchy Reservoir, including its immense dam, and Wapama and Tueeulala Falls. If you visit much later than May or June, you may see only Wapama, the most robust of Hetch Hetchy's waterfalls; Tueeulala dries up early in the year. Although the vista is not perfect from Lookout Point—it would be better if it were 500 feet (150 m) higher—this is still a fine spot to spread out a picnic. You probably won't have any company either.

SMITH PEAK

DISTANCE: 13 miles (20.9 km) round-trip
DURATION: 6 hours
ELEVATION GAIN: 3,700 feet (1,130 m)

Lookout Point (left); Native American grinding holes along the trail to Smith Peak (right)

EFFORT: Very strenuous
TRAILHEAD: Smith Peak
DIRECTIONS: Drive north on Evergreen Road (1 mi/1.6 km west of the Big Oak Flat entrance to Yosemite) for 7.4 miles (11.9 km) and turn right onto Hetch Hetchy Road. Drive 1.5 miles (2.4 km) to the Hetch Hetchy entrance station; then continue 6 miles (9.7 km) to the Smith Peak trailhead on the right side of the road.

This steep and challenging hike will earn you the summit of 7,751-foot (2,363-m) Smith Peak, the highest pinnacle in the Hetch Hetchy area. The peak and part of its trail were hit hard by the **Rim Fire** of 2013, so this is an interesting place for hikers to view the process of regrowth after a forest fire. It will be many years before this region recovers completely, but shrubs and young trees are already greening up the slopes. The summit's panoramic view of Hetch Hetchy Reservoir and the Grand Canyon of the Tuolumne River is still as awesome as ever.

Smith Peak can be accessed from several trailheads, but the shortest trip—still a prodigious 13 miles (20.9 km)—begins at the Smith Peak Trailhead on Hetch Hetchy Road.

From the road, the trail climbs alongside Cottonwood Creek to **Cottonwood Meadow** and then **Smith Meadow** beyond; both can be very wet and boggy until mid-June. Beyond Smith Meadow you'll see the most intense fire devastation: The final 1.5 miles (2.4 km) to the **summit** were completely torched. The peak is covered with pockmarked granite boulders, and its wide summit vista of Hetch Hetchy Reservoir, 4,000 feet (1,220 m) below, as well as the Cathedral and Clark Ranges to the north and east, offers a fine reward for the climb.

★ TUEEULALA AND WAPAMA FALLS

DISTANCE: 4.8 miles (7.7 km) round-trip
DURATION: 2.5-3 hours
ELEVATION GAIN: 350 feet (105 m)
EFFORT: Easy
TRAILHEAD: O'Shaughnessy Dam
DIRECTIONS: From Groveland, drive east on Highway 120 for 22.5 miles (36 km) to the Evergreen Road turn-off, signed for Hetch Hetchy Reservoir (1 mi/1.6 km west of the Big Oak Flat entrance to Yosemite). Drive north on Evergreen Road for 7.4 miles (11.9 km) and turn right onto Hetch Hetchy

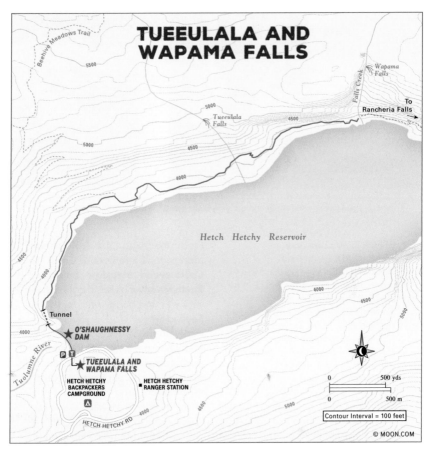

TUEEULALA AND WAPAMA FALLS

Beehive Meadows Trail

5500

Wapama Falls

Falls Creek

To Rancheria Falls

5000

Tueeulala Falls

4500

5000

4500

4000

Hetch Hetchy Reservoir

4500

4000

4000

4500

5000

Tunnel

O'SHAUGHNESSY DAM

4000

Tuolumne River

TUEEULALA AND WAPAMA FALLS

HETCH HETCHY BACKPACKERS CAMPGROUND

HETCH HETCHY RANGER STATION

HETCH HETCHY RD

4000

4500

5000

0   500 yds

0   500 m

Contour Interval = 100 feet

© MOON.COM

Road. Drive 9 miles (14.5 km) to the dam and trailhead.

If you only have time for one hike in Hetch Hetchy, walk across the dam and through the tunnel to access the trail to Tueeulala and Wapama Falls. This short hike is best in spring, when the waterfalls are gushing, but at any time it provides great views of the reservoir and Hetch Hetchy's granite formations.

In the spring and early summer months, two waterfalls are visible from O'Shaughnessy Dam: Tueeulala and Wapama Falls. Both falls drop about 1,000 feet (300 m) before they hit the waterline of Hetch Hetchy

Reservoir, which means they were nearly 1,800 feet (550 m) high before the great human-created flood. By July, wispy Tueeulala Fall usually runs dry, but Wapama keeps a fair flow going into August. In spring, Wapama Fall sometimes runs with such force that the National Park Service is forced to close the trail below it. A 4.8-mile (7.7-km) round-trip hike leads from the dam to the falls.

The trail to these falls starts by crossing the giant **O'Shaughnessy Dam.** After passing through a lighted 500-foot-long (150-m) tunnel, the trail opens out to a mixed forest along the edge of the deep-blue lake. Wildflower displays are often

trail to Tueeulala Fall

excellent in late spring. In 1.5 miles (2.4 km) you reach **Tueeulala Fall,** a delicate wisp of a freefall that only runs during peak snowmelt and is often dry by late May. Less than 1 mile (1.6 km) farther, you reach powerful **Wapama Fall** on Falls Creek, a Bridalveil-like plume of white water that makes a dramatic plunge into the reservoir. Depending on how early in the year you visit, you may get soaking wet standing on the sturdy steel bridges that cross over Wapama Fall's coursing flow.

BEEHIVE MEADOW TRAIL

DISTANCE: 6 miles (9.7 km) round-trip
DURATION: 3-4 hours
ELEVATION GAIN: 1,200 feet (365 m)
EFFORT: Moderate
TRAILHEAD: O'Shaughnessy Dam
DIRECTIONS: Drive north on Evergreen Road (1 mi/1.6 km west of the Big Oak Flat entrance to Yosemite) for 7.4 miles (11.9 km) and turn right onto Hetch Hetchy Road. Drive 9 miles (14.5 km) to the dam and trailhead.

Pick a cool day in spring or fall to travel this exposed sunny-slope trail that switchbacks uphill from Hetch Hetchy Reservoir and provides breathtaking bird's-eye views. From the trailhead at O'Shaughnessy Dam, walk 1 mile (1.6 km) along the edge of Hetch Hetchy Reservoir to the turnoff for Beehive Meadow Trail, which heads north and away from the lake. The trail follows an old road bed through a series of switchbacks, climbing 1,200 feet (365 m) over the course of 2 miles (3.2 km) to the canyon rim. This makes a nice turnaround point for a 6-mile (9.6-km) round-trip with spectacular views. In springtime, this trail also offers a fantastic display of wildflowers.

★ CARLON FALLS

DISTANCE: 4 miles (6.4 km) round-trip
DURATION: 2 hours
ELEVATION GAIN: 350 feet (105 m)
EFFORT: Easy
TRAILHEAD: Carlon Day Use Area

bridge crossing Wapama Fall

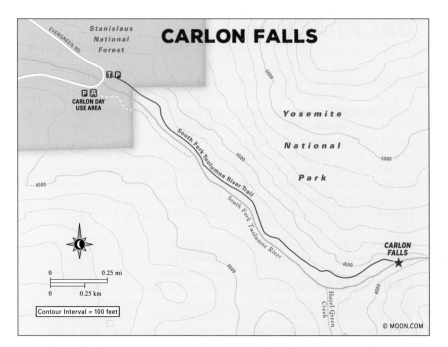

CARLON FALLS

Stanislaus National Forest

EVERGREEN RD.

CARLON DAY USE AREA

South Fork Tuolumne River Trail

South Fork Tuolumne River

Yosemite

National

Park

CARLON FALLS

Hazel Green Creek

5000

4500

5000

4500

4500

4500

4500

4800

0   0.25 mi

0   0.25 km

Contour Interval = 100 feet

© MOON.COM

DIRECTIONS: Drive north on Evergreen Road (1 mi/1.6 km west of the Big Oak Flat entrance to Yosemite) for 1 mile (1.6 km) to the far side of the bridge, just past Carlon Day Use Area. Park in the pullout on the right. Begin hiking on the closed-off road, heading upstream.

Carlon Falls is not located in Hetch Hetchy Valley; its trailhead is found on the road to Hetch Hetchy, Evergreen Road. This means it gets missed not just by the large number of Yosemite visitors who never see Hetch Hetchy, but also by visitors who are heading so intently to Hetch Hetchy that they ignore everything along the way. This waterfall on the South Fork Tuolumne River shouldn't be passed by. It has two big factors going for it: It's accessible by an easy, nearly level, pleasant hike; and it's a river waterfall, so it has a dependable amount of flow even in autumn, when Hetch Hetchy's and Yosemite's waterfalls have all but gone dry.

Follow the obvious trail on the north side of the river from Carlon Day Use Area (the trail on the south side is an unmaintained anglers' route). Although you begin your hike in Stanislaus National Forest, you will soon walk into Yosemite National Park. The trail passes through an impressive old-growth pine and fir forest, highlighted by wildflowers in the spring and colorful oak and dogwood leaves in the autumn. After 2 miles (3.2 km) of riverside meandering, you'll reach 30-foot (9-m) **Carlon Falls,** a lacy cascade that drops over a granite ledge in the river. The pool below the falls is deep enough for a swim. The rocks below the falls make a fine picnic spot. The waterfall's namesakes are Dan and Donna Carlon, who operated the popular Carl Inn from 1916 to 1930 near what is now Carlon Day Use Area.

BACKPACKING

If you're hoping for an early-season backpacking trip—April, May, or June—when Yosemite's high country is still blanketed in snow, Hetch Hetchy is your best bet. This region is known for its hot summer temperatures, but in the spring months, the air temps are comfortable, the trails are open, and the wildflowers are blooming in full glory. And a bonus: Permits are almost always easy to come by. **Smith Peak** is not only a day hike (page 178), but also a backpacking trip in this area.

RANCHERIA FALLS
13-27 miles (20.9-43 km) round-trip
There's no better time than spring to hike along the northern edge of Hetch Hetchy Reservoir (elevation 3,796 ft/1,157 m) and admire the three stunning waterfalls—Tueeulala, Wapama, and Rancheria—along the way. An easy overnight backpacking trip leads to the eastern edge of the reservoir and Rancheria Falls (6.5 mi/10.5 km). Beware that the bears in this area are some of the boldest in all of Yosemite; bear canisters are required.

O'Shaughnessy Dam is the trailhead for Rancheria Falls. The trail to the Rancheria Falls backpackers' camp is mostly level, with a total elevation gain of only 1,300 feet (400 m) spread over 6.5 miles (10.5 km). This makes it manageable even for most beginners. Fishing in the reservoir is fair to middling in spring and fall. And remember: Swimming is not allowed in this public water supply.

More adventurous backpackers will continue past Rancheria to **Tiltill Valley,** 3 miles (4.8 km) farther. **Vernon Lake** lies a half-day's hike beyond (another 6.5 mi/10.5 km). The granite-backed lake is popular with those who tote along fishing gear in the hope of inviting a few rainbow trout to dinner. Good campsites can be found on Falls Creek (permits required) and also near the lake. Take this trip in the early season, however, because the route through Tiltill Valley is notoriously hot and dry in summer. You can easily turn this into a 27-mile (43-km) loop by heading back via Beehive Meadow and Laurel Lake and then hiking south to Hetch Hetchy.

BIKING

HETCH HETCHY ROAD
18 mi (29 km) round-trip
Road bikers looking for a challenging ride can pedal from Evergreen Lodge or Camp Mather to Hetch Hetchy Reservoir on Hetch Hetchy Road. The route is easy enough on the way in, but the climb back out offers one heck of a workout. Even though plenty of cars utilize this road, they don't cause much of a hazard to cyclists because the narrow, winding thoroughfare forces them to keep their speed down.

FOREST SERVICE ROAD 1S02
14-30 mi (22.5-48 km) round-trip
For a ride on smooth pavement, from Evergreen Lodge pedal 0.5 mile

(0.8 km) north on Evergreen Road to Camp Mather. Go left on Forest Service Road 1S02, signed for Cherry Lake. The narrow paved road follows a nearly level contour high above the Tuolumne River Canyon, offering wide views and colorful wildflower displays. At 7 miles (11.3 km), the road intersects with **Cherry Lake Road.** Retrace your tire tracks here, or turn left and continue 8 miles (12.9 km) to the waterfall and swimming hole at **Rainbow Pool.**

CAMPING

There are no developed campgrounds within park boundaries in the Hetch Hetchy region of Yosemite. The Hetch Hetchy **backpackers' campsites** (no reservations) are designated for those beginning or ending a wilderness trip. Campers who wish to stay in these sites may do so for only one night before or after their backpacking trip, and they must have their **wilderness permit** in hand. The sites are walk-in only, and only backpacking equipment may be brought in.

Camp Mather
35250 Mather Road, Groveland; 415/831-2715 or 209/379-2284; www. sfrecpark.org; mid-June-mid-Sept.
A summer camp owned and operated by the City of San Francisco, Camp Mather is just outside the park boundary, 1.5 miles (2.4 km) south of the Hetch Hetchy entrance to Yosemite. If you're a resident of San Francisco (or a very lucky non-resident), you may be able to win the reservation lottery and reserve a week's stay. Residents get top priority in the lottery ($100 fee), which opens in early January and ends in early February each year. The family-friendly camp consists of 100 rustic **cabins** ($457-1,222 per week) that sleep up to six people along with 20 **tent sites** ($247-333 per week).

Bathhouses provide water and laundry services. A meal plan purchase ($20-38 per day) is also required.

Dimond O
34660 Evergreen Road, Groveland; 209/379-2258 or 877/444-6777; www.recreation.gov; June-Oct.; $30
Much of the national forest surrounding Dimond O (36 sites) was badly burned in the Rim Fire of 2013, but the camp and its immediate surroundings were mostly spared, and this is still a lovely spot for an overnight. It's just far enough off the highway that it's peaceful and quiet, but it's still only about 15-20 minutes from Yosemite's Big Oak Flat entrance. Dimond O makes a convenient choice if you plan to visit Hetch Hetchy (10.5 mi/16.9 km away).

flowers by Hetch Hetchy Road

Dimond O's sites are reservable June-October. The camp has drinking water and vault toilets; small trailers and RVs are fine here. The 4,400-foot (1,300-m) elevation makes for pleasant temperatures, even on the hottest days. Dimond O is 5.6 miles (9 km) north of Highway 120 on Evergreen Road.

FOOD AND LODGING

There are no accommodations or restaurants within park boundaries in the Hetch Hetchy region of Yosemite. Evergreen Lodge is located outside the park, but it's on the route between Hetch Hetchy and Yosemite Valley.

Evergreen Lodge
33160 Evergreen Road, Groveland; 209/379-2606 or 800/935-6343; www.evergreenlodge.com
Nine miles (14.5 km) from the Big Oak Flat entrance and about halfway up the road to Hetch Hetchy, Evergreen Lodge is a convenient place to stay for visiting either Yosemite's high country or Hetch Hetchy's spectacular water-filled valley. You can spend a comfortable night in your cabin and then get up early and head to the trailhead at Hetch Hetchy's impressive dam, or drive into the main part of the park and cruise over to Tuolumne Meadows and Tioga Pass. Yosemite Valley is about an hour away. The lodge can accommodate about 300 people at any one time, and on most summer nights, the resort is completely booked.

The lodge's original 16 one- and two-bedroom **cabins,** which date to the 1920s, sit side by side with 72 brand-new cabins, mostly duplexes. All of the cabins ($225-345) have custom-designed "woodsy" interiors, plus modern features like satellite radio. Those looking for a lower-priced overnight option can stay in one of 16 **"custom campsites"** ($130-165 in summer), which come furnished with tents, mattresses, sleeping bags, and pillows; all you need to bring is your toothbrush.

The **Evergreen Lodge Restaurant** (7am-10:30am, noon-3pm, and 5:30pm-10pm daily summer, shorter hours in winter, $14-32) is worth a stop whether you're staying here or not. The menu changes often, but frequent highlights include wild boar tenderloin, grilled flatiron steak, elk tenderloin, and wild Alaskan salmon. An outdoor dining patio adds more summertime seating options. You can also enjoy a meal (and a specialty cocktail menu) at Evergreen's Tavern, open daily from 12 noon until "late," and at the poolside bar in the summer months.

BEST PICNIC SPOTS
There are no designated picnic areas at Hetch Hetchy Reservoir, but when you hike the shoreline trail to **Wapama Fall,** you'll find an array of huge granite slabs that are perfect spots to nosh on a sandwich while you admire the scenery.

Carlon Day Use Area
Evergreen Road, 1 mile (1.6 km) north of Highway 120; $10
Carlon Day Use Area has a beautiful, shady location alongside the South

Carlon Day Use Area (left); Middle Fork Day Use Area (right)

Fork Tuolumne River. You can have a picnic by the river, fish for trout, or walk the old dirt trail from Carlon Road into Yosemite National Park, or follow the longer trail across the river to Carlon Falls. Picnic tables and grills are found on the west side of Evergreen Road; the east side is a more primitive fishing area.

Middle Fork Day Use Area
Evergreen Road, 5 miles (8.1 km) north of Highway 120
Middle Fork Day Use Area on the Middle Fork Tuolumne River is another scenic spot for a rustic picnic. This stretch of the river is popular with anglers fishing for rainbow trout, but there's plenty of space to claim your own river pool and spread out a picnic.

INFORMATION AND SERVICES

It's best to prepare for a trip to Hetch Hetchy by having everything you might need or want already in your car. Opportunities for services, food, and supplies are limited once you leave Highway 120.

Entrance Station
Hetch Hetchy Entrance

The small Hetch Hetchy entrance station lies 9 miles (14.5 km) north of Highway 120 via Evergreen Road and Hetch Hetchy Road. These two roads are sometimes closed during winter storms, but they usually reopen after a few days. Tire chains may be required in winter. Because the roads are narrow and winding, vehicles longer than 25 feet (7.6 m) or wider than 8 feet (2.4 m) are prohibited at all times. Also, note that unlike other roads in the park, the **Hetch Hetchy Road is not open 24 hours a day.** You can drive the road 7am-9pm daily May-Labor Day, with reduced hours the rest of the year, depending on daylight hours.

Visitor Centers

There are no visitor centers in this region of Yosemite, but the ranger at the **Hetch Hetchy entrance station** (Hetch Hetchy Rd.; 209/379-1922) will happily answer any questions.

TRANSPORTATION
Getting There
From Big Oak Flat Entrance

From the Big Oak Flat entrance, head west on Highway 120 for 1 mile (1.6 km) and then turn right on **Evergreen Road** (may be closed in winter). Seven miles (11.3 km) down this road is the **Evergreen Lodge,** a cabin resort with a good restaurant and a store. A half mile (0.8 km) farther is **Camp Mather,** a camp run by the City of San Francisco. Bear right on **Hetch Hetchy Road** (open 7am-9pm daily May-Labor Day, shorter hours in winter, may be closed for brief periods during winter storms) at Camp Mather, and in 1.5 miles (2.4 km) you will pass through the **Hetch Hetchy entrance station** to Yosemite. Get any information you might need here; this is probably your last chance

to see a park ranger. Hetch Hetchy Road continues for another 7.5 winding miles (12.1 km) to **O'Shaughnessy Dam.** The drive from the Big Oak Flat entrance to O'Shaughnessy Dam takes about 30 minutes.

From Yosemite Valley

Hetch Hetchy Reservoir is a 40-mile (64-km) drive from Yosemite Valley via Highway 120 and Evergreen and Hetch Hetchy Roads. Plan on about 75 minutes to make the drive in good weather. Drive out of Yosemite Valley on **Big Oak Flat Road** to the **Big Oak Flat entrance** on Highway 120, which takes about 45 minutes. From there, follow the directions above from the Big Oak Flat entrance.

From Tioga Road

After reaching the western end of Tioga Road at **Crane Flat,** turn right onto **Big Oak Flat Road** to reach the **Big Oak Flat entrance** on Highway 120, about 15 minutes away from Crane Flat. From there, follow the directions from the Big Oak Flat entrance, above.

Driving from Tioga Pass to Hetch Hetchy takes about 2.5 hours.

Parking

Hetch Hetchy is the least visited region of Yosemite, so parking is quite easy most of the year. The exception is during April and May, when the region's waterfalls are flowing and wildflowers are blooming. On weekends and holidays in spring, plan to arrive early to secure a parking space. If the main lot at the dam is full, the ranger at the entrance station will tell you where you can safely and legally park.

Gas and Charging

There is **no gas station** in Hetch Hetchy. The closest gas stations are at **Yosemite Lakes Store** (31191 Hardin Flat Rd.; 209/962-0110), 6 miles (9.7 km) east of the Big Oak Flat entrance station just off Highway 120, and **Crane Flat,** 8 miles (12.9 km) inside the park. The closest charging station is at **Evergreen Lodge,** 1.8 miles (2.9 km) from the Hetch Hetchy entrance. Another charging station is located at **Rush Creek Lodge** on Highway 120, near the junction with Evergreen Road.

A black bear cools off in Hetch Hetchy's reservoir.

BIRDS AND WILDLIFE

Many visitors travel to American national parks in the hopes of seeing wildlife. In this regard, Yosemite often delivers, although you never know which of the park's 76 mammal species, 247 bird species, and 29 reptile and amphibian species will make an appearance at any given time. The following is a brief guide to some of Yosemite's most commonly seen, or most notable, animal denizens.

STELLER'S JAY

Nobody visits Yosemite without seeing the Steller's jay, a bold and raucous bird that makes its presence known. The western cousin of the East Coast's blue jay, the Steller's jay has a distinctive black topknot of feathers that point backward, affording it a regal look. The jay's body is about 10 inches (25 cm) in length and a deep pure blue. When on the ground, the Steller's jay hops—it does not walk. If you are eating a sandwich when one is near, keep a vigilant guard; the jay has no qualms about stealing food. Their nickname is "camp robber."

Where to See Them

- Yosemite Valley picnic areas and campgrounds (page 76 and page 80)

- Wawona picnic areas and campgrounds (page 119)

CLARK'S NUTCRACKER

Similar in size and behavior to the Steller's jay (noisy, cantankerous, and often seen scouting campgrounds and picnic areas for food), the Clark's nutcracker is light gray with white and black patches on its tail and wings. A group of them are often seen and heard among the upper branches of whitebark pine trees, where they quarrel with each other as they collect pine nuts. The bird stores nuts and seeds for the winter in massive granaries, usually located on south-facing slopes. One pair can cache as many as 30,000 nuts and seeds in the fall. In the spring, the birds recall the placement of every single one and retrieve them to feed their young. This high-country bird is easy to spot in the high country of Tioga Pass. You'll usually hear their raucous calls before you see them.

Stellar's jay (top); Clark's nutcracker (middle); pileated woodpecker (bottom)

- Gaylor Lakes (page 152)

WOODPECKER

Plentiful in Yosemite, woodpeckers are frequently seen and heard amid the Valley's tall trees. With some variation, they are all black and white with a dash of flaming red on their heads (although in some species only the males bear the red patch). Anywhere there are lots of trees, you're bound to spot woodpeckers. Most common is the **acorn woodpecker,** which lives in colonies of up to two dozen birds and caches acorns in tree trunks, posts, or other wood structures (sometimes even in the roofs of buildings). A well-stocked granary may hold as many as 10,000 acorns, lined up in neat rows of individually drilled holes. Called el carpintero by the Spanish, the acorn woodpecker prevents marauding squirrels from stealing its stash by pushing the acorns into the holes, pointed end first. The wide end of the acorn sits flush with the surface of the tree trunk, giving squirrels nothing to get their paws on. Acorn woodpeckers can be easily spotted near any snag tree in Yosemite Valley.

The **downy woodpecker,** the smallest woodpecker in North America at about 6 inches (15 cm) long, is also seen in the Valley, usually in streamside forests. In contrast, the **white-headed woodpecker** is seen mostly in pine forests, where it eats pine nuts and insects. White-headed woodpeckers do not drill like most woodpeckers; instead they look for food by pulling bark off trees with their beaks. The white-headed woodpecker is all black except for its white head. The male has a small red head patch.

The **pileated woodpecker,** with a black body, white underwings, and bright red crest, is the largest woodpecker in North America at 16-19 inches (41-48 cm) in length. Its loud, slow drilling can be heard from a mile away under the right conditions (smaller woodpeckers drill with a faster cadence).

Where to See Them

- Mariposa Grove of Giant Sequoias (page 103)
- Merced Grove (page 158)
- Tuolumne Grove (page 142)
- Acorn woodpecker: Cook's Meadow (page 54)
- Pileated woodpeckers: Curry Village (page 82) and above Nevada Fall (page 60)

PEREGRINE FALCON

Having been almost completely wiped out by the pesticide DDT in the 1950s and 1960s, the peregrine falcon is making a comeback in Yosemite and elsewhere, although it is still listed as an endangered species. This remarkable raptor can fly faster than 200 mph (320 km/h). The adult is blue-gray with a whitish breast; its legs and underparts are striped gray. The peregrine falcon nests on the ledges of near-vertical cliffs; several popular rock-climbing sites in Yosemite Valley are closed seasonally to protect nesting sites. When a peregrine falcon hunts, it will circle high until it spots a smaller bird flying below, then plummet downward at breakneck speed and attack it in flight. The female falcon is noticeably larger than the male.

You're unlikely to spot a peregrine falcon without binoculars. Currently there are 14 pairs living in Yosemite,

blue grouse (top); American dipper (middle); great gray owl (bottom)

but they nest high up on extremely sheer cliffs.

Where to See Them (With Binoculars)

- El Capitan (page 51)

BLUE GROUSE

This chicken-like bird is curious and virtually unafraid of humans. Contrary to its name, the grouse is not blue but rather brownish gray. Frequently seen in groups of six or more, the blue grouse pecks at the ground for conifer needles, buds, and seeds. Young grouse are able to walk and feed themselves immediately after they hatch out of their eggs.

Blue grouse are found in any forested area above 6,000 feet (1,800 m). You may hear but not see them while hiking in the high country; the male attracts the female with a strange hooting sound that is amplified by inflating the air sacs on both sides of his neck. The effect sounds something like a hollow drumbeat echoing through the forest ("whoompf"). Note that in 2006, the blue grouse was officially split into two species, the sooty grouse and the dusky grouse. Yosemite grouse are the sooty variety, but most birders have stuck with the name "blue grouse."

Where to See Them

- Glacier Point (page 101)
- May Lake (page 137)

AMERICAN DIPPER

One of John Muir's favorite birds, the dipper (also called the water ouzel) is an unusual songbird often seen amid the spray of waterfalls. Although it is colored a nondescript gray, the dipper lives an extraordinary life,

diving underwater to feed on insects and larvae. The bird has a third eyelid that closes over its eyes to protect it from spray, a flap of skin that closes over its nostrils to keep out water, and an extra-large oil gland that waterproofs its plumage. It often builds its nest behind a waterfall, then flies back and forth through the torrent to feed its young. When searching for food in a stream, it can walk underwater. They can be seen pretty much anywhere there's a stream flowing.

Where to See Them

- Yosemite Falls (page 54)
- Bridalveil Fall (page 55)

GREAT GRAY OWL

An endangered species in California, the great gray owl may be thriving in Yosemite better than anywhere else in the state, although they are at the southernmost end of their habitat range here. The great gray owl is the largest species of North American owl, reaching more than 2 feet (60 cm) tall. It hunts for voles and mice in the daytime as well as at night, usually in meadows surrounded by forest. The great gray owl has a memorable face, with dozens of concentric rings around its small yellow eyes. An estimated 40 great gray owls live within the park's borders.

Where to See Them

- Crane Flat at dusk or early morning (page 142)
- McGurk Meadow (page 107)
- On the fringes of the Wawona Golf Course

BLACK BEAR

The only kind of bear that lives in Yosemite, or anywhere in California, is the black bear. (Although the fearsome grizzly bear once roamed the state and is immortalized on the California flag, grizzlies have been extinct in Yosemite since 1895.) Black

black bear

bears have a somewhat misleading name, as they are commonly brown, blond, or cinnamon-colored—rarely pure black. Often they have a white patch on their chest. The smallest of all North American bears, they typically weigh up to 400 pounds (180 kg); one captured Yosemite bear weighed a whopping 690 pounds (315 kg). They can run up to 30 mph (48 km/h) and are powerful swimmers and climbers. Despite the adult bear's enormous size, bear cubs weigh only half a pound (230 g) at birth. They can be seen in any forested area between 4,000 and 8,000 feet (1,220-2,440 m) elevation.

Black bears will eat just about anything, but their staple foods are berries, fruits, plants, insects, honeycomb, the inner layer of tree bark, fish, and small mammals. Contrary to popular belief, black bears do not hibernate. A pregnant female will "den up" in winter and usually give birth while she is sleeping, but this is not true hibernation. Male black bears are often out roaming for food in winter.

Where to See Them (At a Distance)

- Crane Flat (page 142)
- Yosemite Valley (page 39)
- Wawona (page 89)

Bear Safety

There's only one important fact to remember about California's bears: They love snacks. The average black bear must eat 20,000 calories a day to sustain its body weight. Because its natural diet is made up of berries, fruits, plants, fish, and insects, the high-calorie food of human beings seems very appealing to a bear. A box full of candy bars is a lot easier to swallow than 1,500 acorns.

Campers have trained bears to crave the taste of corn chips, hot dogs, and soda pop. As a result, bears have become less wild, more aggressive, and largely unafraid of humans. Some bears will break into cars and buildings in the hope of finding food, and they teach their young the same bad habits. Ultimately, in the conflict between bears and people, bears lose. Once a bear has developed a taste for human food, there is no turning back. Transporting the bear to another area is ineffective, so bears that develop a reputation as "problem bears" are put to death.

FOOD STORAGE

Any time you see a bear, it's most likely looking for food. It's essential to keep human food packed away in bearproof storage containers when camping or staying in more rustic lodgings, like tent cabins, which bears can easily break into. The brown metal **bearproof boxes** should be closed and latched at all times.

Storing food or any item with a scent that a bear might mistake for food (soap, cosmetics, perfume, insect repellent, sunscreen, empty bottles of soda) in your car is asking for trouble. Bears are remarkably strong, and they can use their claws and muscles to "peel back" car windows and doors.

Backpackers should always use plastic **bear canisters** to store their food for overnight trips. Hanging food from a tree is ineffective and illegal in Yosemite. You can borrow, rent, or buy a bear canister in the park (at the Mountain Shop at Curry Village, Yosemite Valley Wilderness

Center, Tuolumne Meadows Store, Wawona Store, Crane Flat Store, and the Hetch Hetchy entrance station). Canisters can be rented for $5 per trip and can be returned at various locations in the park.

To report improper food storage, trash problems, or other bear-related trouble, call the **Bear Management Team** (209/372-0322). Your call can be made anonymously, and it may save the life of a bear.

DRIVING

Humans are also a menace to bears because we often drive too fast on mountain roads. From 2010 to 2020, an average of 14 bears were killed on park roads each year, although the actual number is probably higher; bears hit by cars often lumber off into the forest, injured, and die a day or two later. Red "bear markers" have been placed alongside roads in spots where bears have been recently hit to remind drivers to slow down.

BEAR ENCOUNTERS

When you are hiking, bears will most likely hear you coming and avoid you. Black bears very rarely harm human beings, but you should never approach or feed a bear, or get between a bear and its cubs or its food. If provoked, a bear could cause serious injury. If a bear approaches while you are eating, yell at it to scare it away, and pick up all your food and walk away with it. Bears respect possession and will not take food away from you. If a bear approaches your campsite, yell, throw small rocks or pinecones, and generally be as obnoxious as possible. A bear that is afraid of humans is a bear that will stay wild and stay alive.

MULE DEER

Frequently seen in Yosemite Valley and crossing roads elsewhere in the park, the mule deer is one of our largest American deer and can weigh up to 450 pounds (200 kg). The deer gets its name from its ears, which are large and rounded. Mule deer in the Sierra have a white patch on their rumps and a black-tipped tail. The antlers on the bucks, which develop in summer, are usually an

mule deer (top); golden-mantled ground squirrel (bottom)

yellow-bellied marmot

elegant matched set of four points on each side.

Where to See Them

- Yosemite Valley (page 39)
- Tuolumne Meadows (page 140)
- Crane Flat (page 142)

SQUIRRELS

The number and variety of squirrels and their close relations in Yosemite can be quite daunting to the amateur naturalist trying to identify them. One of the easiest-to-spot species is the golden-mantled ground squirrel, a common sight at elevations above 6,000 feet (1,800 m). Frequently mistaken for large chipmunks, these cute squirrels can be correctly identified by the fact that they lack the chipmunk's facial stripe. Otherwise, they look much the same, with one white stripe on each side of their brown bodies, bordered by a heavy black stripe. The golden-mantled ground squirrel must fatten itself up all summer to prepare for winter hibernation.

The western gray squirrel is the common gray-coated squirrel we see throughout California, with a long bushy tail and white belly. Western gray squirrels are great tree climbers and are mostly seen below 6,000 feet (1,800 m) elevation. In contrast, the Douglas squirrel (also called a chickaree) is much smaller than the western gray, and colored a mix of brown and gray. This constantly chattering and highly active squirrel is a key player in the giant sequoia forest, where it cuts thousands of seed-bearing cones per hour from the high branches of a sequoia. The cones drop to the ground, the chickaree scrambles down the tree and gnaws on their meat, and the sequoia seeds fall to the earth to regenerate.

Two additional types of ground squirrels are also seen in Yosemite, and both types hibernate in winter. The Belding ground squirrel is a high-country dweller that is brown or gray with a reddish tail; it is often spotted in meadows standing upright on its back legs. The California ground squirrel is seen at lower elevations and is best identified by a silver V-shaped pattern on the shoulders of its brown-spotted coat.

Where to See Them

- Yosemite Valley (page 39)
- Tuolumne Meadows (page 140)
- Douglas squirrel: Mariposa Grove of Giant Sequoias (page 103), Tuolumne Grove (page 142), Merced Grove (page 158)

YELLOW-BELLIED MARMOT

This largest and most curious member of the squirrel family is frequently seen in Yosemite's high country, particularly in rocky areas along Tioga Road. About 7 inches

(18 cm) tall and as long as 2 feet (60 cm), the bold marmot has no enemies and is frequently seen sunning itself on high boulders. The marmot's coat is buff to brown and its belly characteristically yellow. If you see two or more marmots together, they are often wrestling or chasing each other. You may hear them make a high-pitched whistling sound.

Where to See Them

- Olmsted Point (page 137)
- Tuolumne Meadows (page 140)
- Gaylor Lakes (page 152)
- May Lake and Mount Hoffman (page 137)

PIKA

A frequently seen resident in alpine environments higher than 8,000 feet (2,440 m) elevation, the pika is a small relative of the rabbit that busily collects green grasses, then stacks them in the sun and dries them for winter food and insulation. The creature does not hibernate, so it needs to keep a full stock of dried grasses for its winter nourishment. The diminutive pika is most often seen on talus-lined slopes or rocky hillsides; it is easily recognized by its small, rounded ears and the absence of a tail.

Where to See Them

- Olmsted Point (page 137)
- Gaylor Lakes (page 152)

pika

shooting stars

TREES AND FLOWERS

The wide range of elevation and climate in Yosemite produces an incredible variety of flora. The park contains 37 kinds of native trees, from the grand giant sequoia to the delicate dogwood, and 1,400 species of flowering plants.

One of the most rewarding aspects of hiking or driving in Yosemite in the warmer months is seeing the exquisite mosaics of colorful wildflowers. Multihued blooms paint the park's hillsides, peaks, lakeshores, and riverbanks over the course of about six months each year, starting at the lower elevations in March and April. As the high country snow melts, the bloom slowly rises in elevation, until at 10,000 feet (3,000 m) and above, "spring" comes in late July.

All Sierra flora—not just flowers—changes with elevation and occurs in broad bands called life zones. Four main life zones are found in the park: lower montane life zone (Yosemite Valley, Hetch Hetchy Valley, and the stretch of Tioga Road between Big Oak Flat and Crane Flat), upper montane life zone (Glacier Point and along Tioga Road roughly between Crane Flat and Snow Flat), subalpine life zone (between Tuolumne Meadows and Tioga Pass), and alpine life zone (10,500 ft/3,200 m elevation and above).

blooming western dogwood (top); the distinctive bark of a ponderosa pine (middle); cones on a sugar pine (bottom)

GIANT SEQUOIA

The giant sequoia is well known not just for its gargantuan height and girth, which combine to make this tree the largest living thing on earth, but also for its distinctive cinnamon-colored bark. Three native groves of these amazing tree giants exist in Yosemite—Mariposa, Merced, and Tuolumne—and a few planted sequoias live in Yosemite Valley, near The Ahwahnee and at the Yosemite Cemetery.

Where to See Them

- Mariposa Grove of Giant Sequoias (page 103)
- Merced Grove (page 158)
- Tuolumne Grove (page 142)

WESTERN DOGWOOD

One of the showiest tree species of the lower montane life zone is the western dogwood. If you visit Yosemite Valley in May, you will be delighted by the sprays of white blossoms on this small, delicate tree that grows under the canopy of large conifers. The dogwood's 5-inch-wide (13-cm-wide) blooms are not truly flowers, but rather petal-like bracts that surround the true flowers—a dense, yellow cluster in the middle of the bracts. One of the most beautiful evening sights in Yosemite Valley is that of flowering dogwoods lit up by the full moon. The tree also develops attractive red berries in the fall, a favorite food of robins.

Where to See Them

- Carlon Falls (page 182)
- Big Oak Flat Road between the Big Oak Flat entrance station and Crane Flat (page 166)

Mariposa Grove of Giant Sequoias

- Western end of Yosemite Valley near Bridalveil Fall (page 55)

PONDEROSA AND SUGAR PINE

Two common pines of Yosemite Valley can be identified by a few easy-to-remember characteristics. The **ponderosa pine** is recognized by its clearly delineated, jigsaw puzzle-like bark and long needles (4-10 in/10-25 cm). It is often mistaken for the Jeffrey pine, which has similar puzzle-like bark but grows at higher elevations in the upper montane life zone.

The **sugar pine** is the tallest and largest of more than 100 species of pine trees in the world—old trees frequently reach 7 feet (2 m) in diameter and 200 feet (60 m) tall. This venerable pine has unmistakable cones, befitting a tree this size: They are 10-18 inches (25-46 cm) in length, the longest cones of any conifer. The cones hang down like Christmas ornaments off the tips of the sugar pine's long branches. While they are still green, they weigh up to 5 pounds (2.3 kg).

Where to See Them

- Yosemite Valley (page 39)
- Between Big Oak Flat entrance and Crane Flat (page 166)
- Wapama Fall hike (page 179)

INCENSE-CEDAR

The incense-cedar can be identified by its lacy foliage and unusual needles, which are completely flat at the ends, as if they have been ironed. Its bark is shaggy in appearance, and the tree emits a slight spicy odor; some people think its scent is reminiscent of pencils. Like Douglas-fir, the incense-cedar's name is hyphenated because it is not a true cedar.

Where to See Them

- Merced Grove (page 158)
- Tuolumne Grove (page 142)
- Wapama Fall hike (page 179)
- Yosemite Valley (page 39)

WHITE FIR

The sturdy white fir has a white-gray trunk, and the tree commonly reaches a width of 5 feet (1.5 m). It has needles that grow in flat sprays that are distinctly two-dimensional. White firs are easily spotted in Yosemite's three sequoia groves, where their seeds germinate in the thick duff that covers the ground beneath the giant sequoias. Most people recognize white firs because the young ones look like little Christmas trees; indeed, this is a commonly marketed Christmas tree in California. Older trees easily attain heights of 150 feet (45 m).

Where to See Them

- Mariposa Grove of Giant Sequoias (page 103)
- Merced Grove (page 158)
- Tuolumne Grove (page 142)

RED FIR

Red firs are easy to identify because of their reddish-brown bark. They can grow up to 6 feet (1.8 m) in diameter and are seen along the higher elevations of Tioga Road (above 6,000 ft/1,800 m). They often grow in pure groves made up only of their own kind. Depressions at the bases of the biggest trees are sometimes used by bears as winter dens (the same is also true for white firs).

Where to See Them

- Tamarack Flat campground (page 162)
- Cathedral Lakes hike (page 145)

LODGEPOLE PINE

Lodgepole pines are the only two-needled pines in the Sierra. They earned their name because Native Americans used their dependably straight trunks as poles for their tepees and lodges. On Tioga Road, especially near Tuolumne Meadows, lodgepole pines do not grow very tall—most are in the 20- to 40-foot (6-12-m) range. Throughout history the tree has been mistakenly called a tamarack, which is actually a deciduous conifer that does not live anywhere in the Sierra. The lodgepole pine's mistaken identity is the reason for place-names such as Tamarack Lakes and Tamarack Flat that we find in Yosemite and beyond.

Currently, lodgepole pines along and near Tioga Road are suffering from an attack by the **needleminer moth,** an insect whose larvae obtain food and shelter by hollowing out the lodgepole pine's needles. This ultimately kills the tree, and large stands of pines in the Yosemite high country are dead or dying from this insect's activities. However, because the attack of the needleminer moth is a natural occurrence that happens every 100 years or so in a lodgepole pine forest, the National Park Service is allowing Mother Nature to run her course. In the long term, the moth may actually be good for the lodgepole pine forest because it takes out some of the older trees and allows younger, healthier stands to grow in their place.

incense-cedar needles (top); white fir cones (middle); red fir (bottom)

lodgepole pine (top); Jeffrey pine (middle); mountain hemlock (bottom)

Where to See Them

- May Lake (page 137)
- Cathedral Lakes hike (page 145)
- Tamarack Flat campground (page 162)
- White Wolf campground (page 161)
- Tuolumne Meadows campground (page 162)

JEFFREY PINE

The Jeffrey pine is a favorite of many Sierra tree lovers because of the unique scent of its bark, which smells quite sweet, like vanilla or butterscotch. Hungry hikers sometimes liken the smell of the Jeffrey pine to a breakfast of pancakes and maple syrup. The side of the pine that is warmed by sunlight generally emits the strongest scent. Sometimes the odor is so strong it wafts to you from several feet away; other times you must put your nose right up to the tree's bark crevices to smell it.

Like the ponderosa pine, the Jeffrey has jigsaw-puzzle bark. It's especially pronounced on older, wider trees. The two species are sometimes confused, but if you know at what elevation the tree sits, you can usually identify it correctly. Jeffrey pines are rarely seen below 6,000 feet (1,800 m), and ponderosa pines are rarely seen above that elevation. The Jeffrey pine is a rugged tree often seen growing on high granite domes and slopes, seemingly without the aid of soil. A very famous and much-photographed Jeffrey once lived on top of the bald summit of Sentinel Dome in Yosemite, but it finally died of old age in 1979. Other Jeffrey pines still eke out a wind-sculpted living on the dome's bald surface.

Another unique feature of the Jeffrey pine is that its cones are not prickly to the touch because their spines point downward, not outward. This feature has earned the tree the nickname "gentleman Jeffrey." The ponderosa pine's cones, by way of contrast, can be remembered as "prickly ponderosa."

Where to See Them

- Sentinel Dome (page 107)
- Pothole Dome (page 139)
- May Lake trail (page 137)

MOUNTAIN HEMLOCK

The mountain hemlock is easily identified by its uppermost branches, which droop downward or sideways, as if they are taking a bow. Naturalist John Muir was a great fan of the mountain hemlock and wrote a lengthy ode to it in his first book, *The Mountains of California*. The hemlock has greenish-blue foliage that is distinct when viewed close up; its needles are dense and completely cover the stems they grow on, like a coat of fur.

Where to See Them

- Tioga Road between Tenaya Lake and Tioga Pass (page 141)
- Cathedral Lakes hike (page 145)

WESTERN JUNIPER

Western juniper (also called Sierra juniper) is another distinctive Sierra tree, and an easy one to identify because of its bluish-green scale-like needles and its spiraling trunk, which makes it appear as if the tree twisted in circles as it grew. The roots of this hardy tree will tunnel through crevices in granite, making it seem as if the western juniper is growing right out of rock. Western junipers in Yosemite and elsewhere in the Sierra can live as long as 2,000 years. As the juniper ages, its trunk becomes stripped of bark and bleached to a light blond. The juniper produces an abundance of blue "berries" in the summer months, which are well loved by birds. These are actually not berries at all, but the juniper's cones.

Where to See Them

- Olmsted Point (page 137)
- Tioga Road just east of Tenaya Lake (page 141)

Bigelow's sneezeweed (left); cassiope (right)

BIGELOW'S SNEEZEWEED

A member of the aster family, this bright yellow flower attracts a variety of pollinators—hummingbirds, butterflies, and bees. Despite its name, it doesn't cause allergies, but it was once used as snuff. Find it in Yosemite's moist mid-elevation meadows.

Where to See Them

- Crane Flat (page 142)
- Hodgdon Meadow campground (page 162)

CASSIOPE

John Muir wrote lovingly of the white bell-shaped flowers of cassiope, which he described as "the most beautiful and best loved of the heathworts . . . ringing her thousands of sweet-toned bells." This low-growing white heather, usually about 4 inches (10 cm) high, grows in subalpine and alpine environments, often around rocky lakeshores in late-snowmelt areas. Find them at any of the high-alpine lakes near Tioga Pass.

Where to See Them

- Cathedral Peak (page 145)
- Gaylor Lakes (page 152)

ALPINE COLUMBINE

This white variety of Sierra Columbine—sometimes tinged with a pale yellow, pink, or purple—is found only in high-alpine habitats, typically 10,000 feet (3,000 m) or above. It's pollinated by hawk moths, large moths with remarkably long tongues.

Where to See Them

- Tioga Pass (page 142)

alpine columbine (top); crimson columbine (middle); California coneflower (bottom)

CRIMSON COLUMBINE

This handsome red and gold columbine is easy to spot at lower elevations in early summer or in later months at higher elevations, like along Glacier Point Road. This flower's nectar was a sweet treat for Native Americans. Unlike the alpine columbine, this columbine is pollinated by hummingbirds.

Where to See Them

- The Ahwahnee in early summer (page 82)

CALIFORNIA CONEFLOWER

These showy plants grow as tall as 3 feet (1 m) and are topped off with sunflower-like petals surrounding a distinctively long central cone.

Where to See Them

- Crane Flat gas station (page 167)

ELEPHANT HEADS

Get down on your hands and knees so you can make out the elephantine "trunk" and floppy "ears" of this tiny, charming flower. Elephant heads grow in masses in cool, wet meadows above 6,000 feet (1,800 m).

Where to See

- Tuolumne Meadows in July (page 140)

HETCH HETCHY MONKEYFLOWER

California boasts more than 60 species of monkeyflower—in shades ranging from yellow to pink to purple to red—and half of them can be seen in Yosemite. None are quite as stunning as the Hetch Hetchy monkeyflower with its magenta-pink blossoms highlighted by bright yellow splashes. This rare plant is often spotted in areas that have recently burned in wildfires.

elephant heads

Where to See Them

- Wapama Fall hike (page 179)

LEOPARD LILY

This graceful orange lily grows in colonies, so where you'll find one, you'll likely find a few more. Its flowers drape from the top of tall, stout stems growing as tall as 5 feet (1.5 m). Two varieties are almost identical in color and markings, but one has a globe-shaped flower and the other is more fluted (alpine lily). Find these lilies along shady stream banks or on the edge of wet meadows.

Where to See Them

- Wawona Meadow, south side (page 115)

MARIPOSA LILY

Mariposa is the Spanish word for butterfly—the flower's resemblance to these lovely winged creatures suggested the name. Three petals—most often white, but sometimes pink or purple—form a 2-inch-wide (5-cm-wide) cup. These elegant flowers prefer dry, gravelly locations at low to mid-elevations. The roasted bulbs were important food for Yosemite's Indigenous people.

Where to See Them

- Chinquapin (page 105)
- Tunnel View (page 51)

LUPINE

Of the 70 species of lupine that grow in California, more than two dozen are found in Yosemite. Tall, bush-like Gray's lupine, also known as Sierra lupine, can be seen flowering profusely alongside Highway 41 near Wawona in June. Low-growing Brewer's lupine is found at higher

mariposa lily (top); lupine (middle); whorled penstemon (bottom)

elevations. A dazzling pink-and-yellow harlequin lupine grows along the shoreline of Hetch Hetchy. All lupines thrive in soil that is low in nitrogen, so they flourish after wildfires.

Where to See Them

- Highway 41 near Wawona (page 124)
- Hetch Hetchy Reservoir (page 177)
- Middle Gaylor Lake (page 152)

PENSTEMON

More than 200 species of penstemon grow in the West, their tubular flowers in various shades of purples, blues, and reds. Gay penstemon (aka mountain blue penstemon) is one of only a few blue-colored California wildflowers. Along the higher elevations of Tioga Road, magenta-colored mountain pride penstemon grows in granite cracks.

Where to See Them

- West of El Capitan Meadow (page 51)
- White Wolf campground (page 161)

WHORLED PENSTEMON

The whorled penstemon is easily identifiable by the way its flowers "whirl" around its stems. Each stalk supports about a half-dozen whorls of tubular flowers.

Where to See Them

- Tuolumne Meadows (page 140)
- Sunrise Lakes in July (page 145)

PHLOX

The alpine life zone, at the high

phlox (top); pussypaws (middle); red heather (bottom)

elevation of 10,500 feet (3,200 m) and above, is where you'll find phlox, in cushions or mats of colorful flowers. One of the first alpine flowers to bloom, spreading phlox forms a cheerful white or pink carpet in and around rocky outcrops. It often makes an appearance just after the high-elevation snow melts in June. Look for it on granite slabs along Glacier Point Road and on top of Sentinel Dome.

Where to See Them

- Glacier Point (page 101)
- Sentinel Dome (page 107)

PUSSYPAWS

Watch for pussypaws (purslane) in sandy soils at 5,000 feet (1,500 m) and above, like along the trails of Glacier Point Road or the lower elevations of Tioga Road. Pussypaws "moves" according to changes in its internal water pressure. On sunny afternoons, you'll find it with its stems lifted an inch or two above the earth. Come back in the evening, and it will have flattened out on the ground.

Where to See Them

- Sentinel Dome Trail (page 107)
- Taft Point Trail (page 109)

RED HEATHER

On the shores of alpine lakes, large patches of pinkish-red heather cling to the banks. Their small narrow leaves look like fir needles and make a nice green ground cover long after the flowers are finished. Look for red heather at May Lake or Young Lakes.

Where to See Them

- May Lake (page 137)
- Young Lakes (page 155)

scarlet gilia (top); snow plant (middle); western mountain aster (bottom)

SCARLET GILIA

This brightly colored flower, sometimes called skyrocket because of its shape (an elongated tube that seems to burst into its petals) grows in sandy soil and full sun at mid-elevations. Its color varies from a deep scarlet to pink to coral to nearly white.

Where to See Them

• Pohono Trail (page 109)

• Carlon Falls Trail (page 182)

SHOOTING STARS

This member of the primrose family grows en masse in wet meadows and bogs. Its flowers droop downward off curved stems, looking a bit like comets with tails blazing in their wake. They're pollinated by bees that "grab" the flowers and vibrate their wings at a frequency that shakes the pollen loose.

Where to See Them

• Dog Lake (page 155)

SNOW PLANT

In early spring, there's no way to miss this bright red stunner poking up from the ground in shady forested areas. Snow plant is a parasitic species that doesn't have any green parts (chlorophyll). Since it can't get nutrition through photosynthesis, it feeds on soil fungi.

Where to See Them

• Crane Flat (page 142)

• Taft Point Trail (page 109)

WESTERN MOUNTAIN ASTER

This purple flower with a yellow center, called either mountain aster or mountain daisy, grows on stalks about a foot high in large groupings. It ranges widely over meadows in July, its leaves being so slender that they appear to be blades of grass.

Where to See Them

• McGurk Meadow (page 107)

WESTERN WALLFLOWER

Make sure you bend over and put your nose to this golden flower—its beguiling scent is worthy of savoring. A member of the mustard family, wallflower grows in mid-elevation regions. Look for it wherever there are sunny, dry patches in the forest. At higher elevations, the flower is more yellow; at lower elevations, it's more orange.

Where to See Them

• Crane Flat (page 142)

a butterfly on a western wallflower

Cathedral Rocks in Yosemite Valley

ESSENTIALS

GETTING THERE

The vast majority of Yosemite visitors enter the park in a private automobile or RV. Taking public transportation—train and bus—to the park is possible, but it requires a little planning. Once in the park, you will probably want to have a car anyway unless you plan to spend all your time in Yosemite Valley, where free shuttle buses make cars unnecessary.

AIR

Yosemite is within a four-hour drive of the San Francisco Bay Area, a major metropolitan area with three airports. These Bay Area airports offer the most flight options for Yosemite-bound travelers. You can also fly into Sacramento Airport, which is a four-hour drive from Yosemite's northwest entrance. In summer, when Yosemite's eastern entrance at Tioga Pass is open, Reno Airport provides another option—it's three hours from Tioga Pass. Year-round, the closest airport to Yosemite is in Fresno, about two hours from Yosemite's southern entrance.

San Francisco International Airport

SFO; San Francisco; 650/821-8211 or 800/435-9736; www.flysfo.com
DRIVING TIME TO YOSEMITE: 4 hours to Arch Rock entrance or Big Oak Flat entrance (both entrances open year-round)

Oakland International Airport

OAK; 1 Airport Dr., Oakland, CA; 510/563-3300; www.oaklandairport.com
DRIVING TIME TO YOSEMITE: 3.5 hours to Arch Rock entrance or Big Oak Flat entrance (both entrances open year-round)

San Jose International Airport

SJC; 1701 Airport Blvd., San Jose, CA; 408/392-3600; www.flysanjose.com
DRIVING TIME TO YOSEMITE: 3.5 hours to Arch Rock entrance or Big

Oak Flat entrance (both entrances open year-round)

Sacramento International Airport

SMF; 6900 Airport Blvd., Sacramento, CA; 916/929-5411; www.sacairports.org
DRIVING TIME TO YOSEMITE: 4 hours to Arch Rock entrance; 3 hours to Big Oak Flat entrance (both entrances open year-round)

Fresno-Yosemite International Airport

FAT; 5175 E. Clinton Ave., Fresno, CA; 559/621-4500 or 800/244-2359; www.flyfresno.com
DRIVING TIME TO YOSEMITE: 2 hours to South entrance (open year-round)

Reno-Tahoe International Airport

RNO; 2001 E. Plumb Lane, Reno, NV; www.renoairport.com
DRIVING TIME TO YOSEMITE: 3 hours to Tioga Pass entrance (open mid-June-late Oct.)

CAR

Yosemite National Park is on the western slope of the Sierra Nevada, and driving is the primary way visitors reach the park.

Driving Times

- **San Francisco:** 4 hours
- **Los Angeles:** 7 hours
- **Las Vegas:** 6 hours

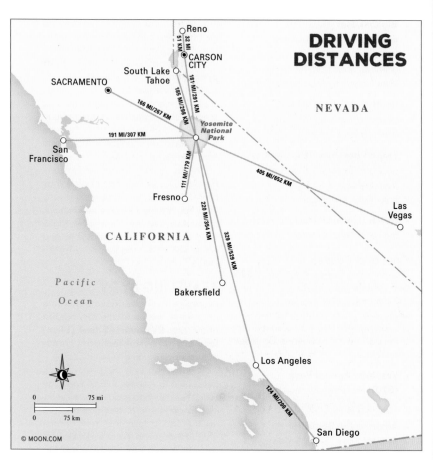

DRIVING DISTANCES

Reno

CARSON CITY

51 MI/81 KM

32 MI/51 KM

South Lake Tahoe

SACRAMENTO

181 MI/291 KM

185 MI/298 KM

166 MI/267 KM

NEVADA

191 MI/307 KM

Yosemite National Park

San Francisco

111 MI/179 KM

405 MI/652 KM

Fresno

Las Vegas

220 MI/354 KM

CALIFORNIA

329 MI/529 KM

Pacific Ocean

Bakersfield

Los Angeles

124 MI/200 KM

San Diego

0   75 mi

0   75 km

© MOON.COM

TRAIN AND BUS
Amtrak
800/872-7245; www.amtrak.com

The nearest Amtrak station is in the town Merced, California, more than an hour's drive from the park. Visitors riding Amtrak need to board a bus or rent a car to continue to Yosemite, but Amtrak makes it relatively easy with a prearranged train-bus package. Bus transportation is available year-round from the Merced Amtrak station to Yosemite on the Amtrak thruway bus, a route that is also served by **YARTS bus service** (Yosemite Area Regional Transportation System; 877/989-2787; www.yarts.com). Travel time is 2.5 hours one-way, and reservations should be made 24 hours in advance.

Greyhound
www.greyhound.com

Greyhound runs bus service to Merced, California, an hour or so west of the park. The regional **YARTS bus service** (Yosemite Area Regional Transportation System; 877/989-2787; www.yarts.com) runs connections between the Merced Greyhound bus stop and Yosemite.

PARK ENTRY
Entrance Stations

Yosemite National Park has five entrance stations:

- **Arch Rock** (Hwy. 140): the main entrance to the park; provides access to Yosemite Valley from the west (San Francisco, Sacramento)

- **Big Oak Flat** (Hwy. 120): provides access to Yosemite Valley and Tuolumne Meadows (summer only) from the north (San Francisco, Sacramento)
- **South** (Hwy. 41): provides access to Wawona from the south (Fresno, Los Angeles)
- **Tioga Pass** (Hwy. 120): provides access to Tuolumne Meadows from the east in summer only (Reno, Las Vegas)
- **Hetch Hetchy:** the only access to the Hetch Hetchy region of the park

Fees and Passes

The entrance fee at Yosemite is **$35 per vehicle** (car, RV, truck, etc.) and $30 per motorcycle. The fee is good for seven days, and you must show your receipt any time you pass through one of the park entrance stations. Other fee options include:

- **Yosemite Annual Pass ($70):** Provides entrance to Yosemite for one year.
- **America the Beautiful Annual Pass ($80):** Provides entrance to all national parks and federal recreation sites in the United States for one year.
- **Senior Lifetime Pass ($80):** Lifetime version of the Interagency Pass for seniors 62 and older. An annual senior pass is also available for $20 per year.

GETTING AROUND
DRIVING

Except on crowded summer days in Yosemite Valley, driving a car around Yosemite National Park is quite easy. More than 200 miles (320 km) of roads lace the park, and parking is not usually difficult (except in Yosemite Valley in summer). If you are visiting Yosemite Valley April-September, consider leaving your car in one of the day-use parking areas and riding the free shuttle bus or taking an organized tour.

Remember always to follow **bear precautions** when leaving your car parked anywhere in Yosemite, especially at night. This means nothing scented should remain inside the car, including food and toiletries. Even an empty soda can or a tube of toothpaste can inspire a bear to break into your car.

When visiting Yosemite November-April, know that **tire chains** may be required on any park road at any time. You are least likely to need chains on Highway 140, the "All-Weather Highway," but it is still always possible, and winter visitors are required to carry tire chains in their cars.

TRAVELING BY RV

Recreational vehicles (RVs) are welcome in Yosemite, except for the very biggest of the rigs: **RVs over 45 feet (14 m) long are not permitted** in most areas of the park, including Yosemite Valley.

Certain roads in the park are not accessible to smaller RVs as well. The Hetch Hetchy Road is closed to all vehicles longer than 25 feet (7.6 m). The access road to Yosemite Creek Campground is closed to RVs or trailers longer than 24 feet (7.3 m), and the road to Tamarack Flat Campground is not recommended for large RVs.

If you are visiting Yosemite Valley for the day in your RV, you would be well advised to enter the park early in the morning, park your rig as soon as possible, and then ride the free Valley shuttle bus to all of the Valley's sites (or join an organized tour, rent a bike and ride, or walk around the Valley on foot).

If you are planning to camp in your RV, know in advance that there are no utility hookups in Yosemite. Park regulations permit the use of generators 7am-7pm only. Dump stations are available at three locations in the park: Upper Pines Campground, Wawona Campground, and Tuolumne Meadows Campground.

PARK SHUTTLES AND PUBLIC TRANSPORTATION

Park Shuttles

Free hybrid shuttle buses run year-round in Yosemite Valley and along a stretch of Tioga Road (Tuolumne Meadows area) in summer. A free shuttle bus also runs from the Mariposa Grove Welcome Plaza to the Mariposa Grove of Giant Sequoias from April to November. Unlike the shuttle buses in the rest of the park, this one is mandatory; it is used to relieve traffic on the Mariposa Grove Road. In winter, a free shuttle runs from Yosemite Valley to Badger Pass.

YARTS Buses

Yosemite Area Regional Transportation System; 877/989-2787; www.yarts.com; $2-30

For visitors staying in towns just outside the park borders, YARTS buses run from some gateway towns outside the park into Yosemite Valley. YARTS buses travel on Highway 120 and Highway 41 (summer only) and Highway 140 (year-round). The bus system provides an option for visitors who would rather not drive and hassle with parking in Yosemite Valley. Ticket prices vary, depending on your departure point. Purchase your ticket online at www.yarts.com or directly from the bus driver.

YARTS buses travel from Merced, Catheys Valley, Mariposa, Midpines, and El Portal to Yosemite Valley along Highway 140; from Mammoth Lakes, June Lake, Lee Vining, and Tuolumne Meadows to Yosemite Valley along Highway 120; from Sonora and Groveland along Highway 120; and from Oakhurst and Fish Camp to Yosemite Valley along Highway 41.

NEAR THE ARCH ROCK ENTRANCE

The Arch Rock entrance, the closest entrance to Yosemite Valley, is approached from the west via Highway 140. A few hamlets lie along Highway 140 within an hour's drive of the Arch Rock entrance: **El Portal** (14 mi/22.5 km from Yosemite Valley), **Midpines** (26 mi/42 km from the Arch Rock entrance), and **Mariposa** (30 mi/48 km from the Arch Rock entrance, 44 mi/71 km from Yosemite Valley). Keep in mind that Highway 140 is a mountain road, not a superhighway, so you won't drive much faster than 45 mph (72 km/h).

Food and Accommodations

EL PORTAL

There are three main lodging options in El Portal: **Yosemite Blue Butterfly Inn** (www.yosemitebluebutterflyinn.com), **Yosemite View Lodge** (www.stayyosemiteviewlodge.com), and **Cedar Lodge** (www.stayyosemitecedarlodge.com). Yosemite View Lodge and Cedar Lodge also have restaurants where nonguests can eat.

MIDPINES

The smaller hamlet of Midpines is 26 miles (42 km) from the Arch Rock entrance to Yosemite. **Yosemite Bug Rustic Mountain Resort** (www.yosemitebug.com) and AutoCamp Yosemite (www.autocamp.com/yosemite) are the main lodging options. Both also have on-site restaurants with delicious food.

MARIPOSA

Mariposa, the county seat for the county of the same name, is a small town at the junction of Highway 140 and Highway 49. The town's six-block-long main street is lined with small shops and restaurants. Mariposa also has several bed-and-breakfasts, inns, and motels, some on the main drag and others spread around the surrounding countryside. Mariposa is the last chance for supplies before driving the final stretch along the flowing Merced River to the Arch Rock entrance.

Information

Mariposa County, which encompasses all three of these communities, offers visitor information on its Yosemite Area Traveler Information site (www.

yosemite.com). Camping, dining, hiking, and other travel information is provided, and the lodging links are especially useful.

For information specifically on local bed-and-breakfasts in the area, contact the **Yosemite-Mariposa Bed and Breakfast Association** (www.yosemitebnbs.org).

NEAR THE BIG OAK FLAT ENTRANCE

Visitors approaching from Sacramento and the San Francisco Bay Area often use the Highway 120 approach through the Big Oak Flat entrance to Yosemite. The towns with services along or near Highway 120 include **Hardin Flat** (along Hardin Flat Road, 5 mi/8 km from the Big Oak Flat entrance), **Buck Meadows** (13 mi/20.9 km from the Big Oak Flat entrance), and the main gateway town of **Groveland** (22 mi/35 km from the Big Oak Flat entrance). From Groveland, the farthest-out town on Highway 120, it's a 45-minute drive to the Big Oak Flat entrance and another 30-45 minutes (20 mi/32 km) to Yosemite Valley along Big Oak Flat Road, so plan on a **75- to 90-minute drive to Yosemite Valley,** depending on traffic and road conditions.

For information on local lodgings, visit the **Stay Near Yosemite** lodging association website (www.staynearyosemite.com). You'll be able to check availability at multiple Groveland-area hotels, cabins, and bed-and-breakfasts simultaneously, which can save you some phone calls. **Buck Meadows** and **Groveland** have the most offerings for places to stay and eat. **Hardin Flat,** while close to the entrance, has a few lodgings but very limited dining options, with the exception of Rush Creek Lodge (www.rushcreeklodge.com).

NEAR THE SOUTH ENTRANCE

Visitors approaching Yosemite from points south, such as Los Angeles and the rest of Southern California, often take Highway 41 to the park's South entrance. There are a few towns with services along the way.

Fish Camp

The old logging town of Fish Camp is on Highway 41, just 2-3 miles (3.2-4.8 km) south of Yosemite's South entrance and right next door to the Yosemite Mountain Sugar Pine Railroad (www.ymsprr.com), a destination especially popular with families.

FOOD AND ACCOMMODATIONS

On the outskirts of Fish Camp you'll find the sprawling **Tenaya at Yosemite** (www.visittenaya.com) resort complex—a large hotel plus cottages and cabins—and multiple smaller lodgings and bed-and-breakfasts. Fish Camp is your best bet for food if you can't find something inside the park. There are three eateries at Tenaya at Yosemite, as well as the **Narrow Gauge Inn** (www.narrowgaugeinn.com).

Oakhurst

As you approach Yosemite from the south, Oakhurst is the last "big town" before the South entrance and the most developed of any of the towns near Yosemite's borders. The town is located at the junction of Highway 41 and Highway 49, about 15 miles (24 km) from the South entrance and 45 miles (72 km) from Yosemite Valley.

FOOD AND ACCOMMODATIONS

This town of about 13,000 inhabitants has several bed-and-breakfasts, inns, motels, and even a spectacular château, **Château du Sureau** (www.chateausureau.com). You can buy pretty much anything in Oakhurst, from hardware to hiking boots to a fancy dinner.

Bass Lake

Bass Lake is 5 miles (8.1 km) east of Oakhurst via Bass Lake Road and 18 miles (29 km) from the South entrance via Highway 41, about a 45-minute drive. While it's a feasible base for visitors who want to spend most of their Yosemite vacation in the southern

part of the park, Bass Lake is about a 90-minute drive to Yosemite Valley.

FOOD AND ACCOMMODATIONS

A stay at Bass Lake fits the bill for anybody who likes boating or fishing. With several campgrounds, restaurants, and resorts, plus numerous places to rent boats or buy fishing equipment, the lakeshore is more like a vacation town than a peaceful mountain retreat.

Information

Managed by Madera County, the **Yosemite Sierra Visitors Bureau** (www.yosemitethisyear.com) has information on lodging, dining, and activities specific to the Highway 41 and Oakhurst-area park gateway.

NEAR THE TIOGA PASS ENTRANCE

Yosemite visitors who exit the park from the eastern Tioga Pass entrance make a precipitous descent over the 13 miles (20.9 km) from the entrance station at 9,945 feet (3,031 m) elevation to the valley floor at U.S. 395 at 6,800 feet (2,070 m). Waiting at the bottom of this spine-tingling drive is the small town of **Lee Vining,** a gateway to the eastern part of Yosemite and rest of the Eastern Sierra. Fifteen miles (24 km) south of Lee Vining lies the popular winter and summer resort town of **June Lake,** which can also serve as a base for Tioga Pass and Tuolumne Meadows visitors.

The closest option for food and lodging outside the Tioga Pass entrance is **Tioga Pass Resort** (Hwy. 120, 2 mi/3.2 km east of Tioga Pass; www.tiogapassresort.com), but the resort has been closed due to extensive weather-related damage since 2017. The owners hope to get this historic enclave of cabins, motel rooms, and a restaurant reopened by 2024.

Lee Vining

Home to Mono Lake, one of the oldest saline lakes in North America, Lee Vining puts you 13 miles (20.9 km) east of the Tioga Pass entrance to Yosemite and near the junction of Highway 120 and U.S. 395. Those miles between the town and Tioga Pass cover one of the most spectacular drives in the West—climbing up through the granite walls of Lee Vining Canyon to 9,945-foot (3,031-m) Tioga Pass.

FOOD AND ACCOMMODATIONS

Lee Vining contains a handful of motels, restaurants, gas stations, and stores—everything the traveler might need for visiting its neighboring world-class attractions.

INFORMATION

Almost anything a traveler might need to know about the area east of Yosemite can be found at **www.monocounty.org,** run by the Mono County Economic Development staff. This site features a ton of information on lodging, activities, trip planning, and more for Lee Vining, June Lake, and other Eastern Sierra towns.

Located on the east side of U.S. 395, just 1 mile (1.6 km) north of Lee Vining, the **Mono Basin Scenic Area Visitor Center** (760/647-3044; 8am-5pm daily Apr.-Nov.) is a great place to stop for recreation and local history information. The smaller **Mono Lake Committee's Information Center and Bookstore** (760/647-6595; www.monolake.org; 8am-9pm daily summer, 9am-5pm daily winter) is right in downtown Lee Vining.

June Lake

The community of June Lake is a full-service resort along Highway 158, just off U.S. 395. Home of world-class trout fishing and myriad opportunities for hiking, biking, camping, and boating, June Lake is a popular vacation destination for visitors who may or may not choose to make the 45-minute trek to the Tioga Pass entrance to Yosemite. Yosemite Valley is too far for a day trip (2.5 hours each way), but much of Yosemite's spectacular high country is within an hour's drive.

FOOD AND ACCOMMODATIONS

This area includes four large drive-to lakes set off a looping highway and provides lodging options at classic mountain cabin resorts, as well as spectacular fishing and hiking. The small town of June Lake has a few excellent eateries and a popular brewery.

INFORMATION

The local chamber of commerce operates two websites with information about the area: **www.junelakeloop.org** and **www.junelakeloop.com**. June Lake information is also available on **www.monocounty.org**.

RECREATION
HIKING

If you have your heart set on climbing Half Dome, you'll need to secure a **Half Dome permit** up to one year in advance. Backpackers should also secure wilderness permits far in advance. Otherwise, the following 10 essentials will help ensure that your outdoor adventures stay safe and fun.

1. Food and water. Water is more important than food, although it's unwise to get caught without at least some edible supplies for emergencies. If you don't want to carry heavy bottles of water, at least carry a purifier or filtering device so that you can obtain water from streams, rivers, or lakes. Never, ever drink water from a natural source without purifying it. Food selections are much-debated matters of personal choice. If you don't want to carry much weight, stick with high-energy snacks like nutrition bars, nuts, dried fruit, turkey or beef jerky, and crackers. If you're hiking in a group, each of you should carry your own food and water just in case someone gets too far ahead or behind.

2. Trail map. Never count on trail signs to get you where you want to go. Signs get knocked down or disappear due to rain, wind, or visitors looking for souvenirs. Carry a map that is much more detailed than the free map provided at park entrance stations. A variety of maps are for sale at park visitor centers and stores. Try maps published by Tom Harrison Maps or National Geographic Trails Illustrated.

3. Extra clothing. Not only can the weather suddenly turn windy, cloudy, or rainy (it can even snow!), but your body's condition also changes: You'll perspire as you hike up a sunny hill and then get chilled at the top of a windy ridge or when you head into shade. Always carry a lightweight, waterproof, wind-resistant jacket. Stay away from clothing made from cotton; once cotton gets wet, it stays wet. Polyester-blend fabrics dry faster; some high-tech fabrics wick moisture away from your skin. In cooler temperatures, or when heading to a mountain summit, carry gloves and a hat as well.

4. Flashlight. Mini-flashlights are available everywhere, weigh almost nothing, and can save the day. Tiny "squeeze" LED flashlights, about the size and shape of a quarter, can clip onto any key ring. Bring two or three. Make sure the batteries work before you set out on the trail.

5. Sunglasses and sunscreen. The higher the elevation, the more dangerous the sun's rays are. Put on high-SPF sunscreen 30 minutes before you go out, and then reapply every 2-3 hours. Protect your face with a wide-brimmed hat and your lips with high-SPF lip balm.

6. Insect repellent. Find one that works for you and carry it with you. Many types of insect repellent use an ingredient called DEET, which is effective but also quite toxic, especially for children. Other types of repellent are made of natural substances, such as lemon or eucalyptus oil. If you visit White Wolf's meadows in the middle of a major mosquito hatch, it may seem like nothing works to repel bugs except covering your entire body in mosquito netting.

7. First-aid kit. Supplies for blister repair, an elastic bandage, an antibiotic ointment, and an anti-inflammatory

medicine such as ibuprofen can be valuable in emergencies. If you're allergic to bee stings or anything else in the outdoors, carry medication.

8. Swiss Army-style pocketknife. Carry one with several blades, a can opener, scissors, and tweezers.

9. Compass. Know how to use it. If you prefer to use GPS, that's fine, but know that GPS may not work everywhere you go.

10. Emergency supplies. Ask, "What would I need if I had to spend the night outside?"

In addition to food and water, these supplies can get you through an unplanned night in the wilderness:

- Purchase a lightweight blanket or sleeping bag made of foil-like Mylar film designed to reflect radiating body heat. These make a great emergency shelter and weigh and cost almost nothing.

- Keep matches and a candle in a waterproof container (or zippered bag), just in case you ever need to build a fire in an emergency.

- Bring a whistle. If you need help, you can blow a whistle for a lot longer than you can shout.

- A flash from a small signal mirror can be seen from far away.

BACKPACKING

Going backpacking in Hetch Hetchy or elsewhere in Yosemite? It's far too easy to head out on the trail and realize too late that you left a critical item at home. Use this handy checklist to help you pack, or tailor it to your own individual needs.

1. Permit. First and foremost, you need a **wilderness permit** (reserve in advance at www.recreation.gov/permits/445859 or learn more about the permit system at www.nps.gov/yose/planyourvisit/wildpermits.htm). If you didn't plan ahead, show up at one of Yosemite's wilderness permit offices and see what permits are still available. You may have to be flexible about what trailhead you use as your starting point, and you may have to wait 24 hours to leave on your trip.

2. Shelter. Tent, rain fly, poles, and stakes, plus a ground tarp (a rain poncho can serve this purpose).

3. Sleeping. Sleeping bag and sleeping pad. If you are a creature of comfort, pack along a small pillow too.

4. Food and cooking. In Yosemite, you must store your food (and any scented items) in a bear canister. This is not just a good idea—it's the law. Buy or rent one at the Hetch Hetchy entrance station or at other locations in Yosemite. To cook and eat, you'll need a camp stove and plenty of fuel, waterproof matches or a lighter, a set of lightweight pots and pans with lids, pot grips for handling hot pots, zip-locking bags, trash bags, lightweight cutlery and dishes, and a cup for drinking. Carry as much freeze-dried or lightweight food as you can (more than you think you'll need). Most important, don't forget a water bottle and filter or some type of purifier like a Steripen ultraviolet light.

5. Clothing. A good basic packing list includes underwear, socks, T-shirts, shorts or convertible pants, a long-sleeved shirt, windproof and waterproof jacket and pants, gloves, hats (both a warm hat for cold nights and mornings and a wide-brimmed hat for sun protection), sunglasses, rain poncho, hiking boots, and lightweight camp shoes or sandals such as Tevas.

6. Toiletries. You can go without a lot in the backcountry, but you don't want to go without sunscreen and sun-protecting lip balm, insect repellent, toothbrush and toothpaste, and maybe a comb or hair bands. Some backpackers bring toilet paper; if you do, remember that you must pack it out. (Minimalists use large leaves instead.) A small plastic trowel is useful for burying human waste.

7. First-aid kit. A basic kit should include an emergency space blanket made of Mylar film, tweezers, sterile

gauze pads, adhesive medical tape, adhesive bandages in assorted sizes, an elastic bandage, aspirin or ibuprofen, moleskin for blisters, antibiotic ointment, and any prescription medications you might need.

8. Other critical stuff. Two or more flashlights and extra batteries, GPS or compass, small signal mirror, appropriate maps, hiking poles, whistle, 50-foot (15-m) nylon cord, candles, extra matches, repair kit or sewing kit, safety pins, and a Swiss Army-style pocketknife.

9. Fun stuff. Camera and memory card, extra camera battery, binoculars, fishing gear and license, pen and pencil, playing cards, star chart, and nature identification guides for birds, flowers, trees, etc.

10. What to put it all in. A backpack, of course. And if the top of your backpack doesn't separate from the main pack to make a day pack, carry along a smaller day pack for taking short outings from your base camp.

Wilderness Permits

A wilderness permit is required **year-round** for any overnight stay in the backcountry areas of Yosemite. (You do not need a permit for day hikes, except for hiking to Half Dome.) Due to the number of people who wish to backpack through Yosemite's backcountry, **quotas** are in effect late April through October for the number of permits granted at all wilderness trailheads. Sixty percent of the daily quota can be reserved up to 24 weeks ahead of time; the remaining 40 percent are available seven days in advance starting at 7am.

Yosemite's wilderness permit system—and the quotas for the number of backpackers who can enter at any trailhead on any given day—may seem complicated, but all the details are found at the Yosemite Wilderness Permit webpage (www.nps.gov/yose/planyourvisit/wildpermits.htm), or you can simply follow the "Reserve a Permit" instructions below.

One more thing: If you think you can sneak off into Yosemite's backcountry without a wilderness permit and not get caught, think again. Especially in the summer months, rangers regularly patrol Yosemite's wilderness areas and check to see that backpackers are carrying permits.

BIKING

Bicycles are available for rent in Yosemite Valley—at **Yosemite Valley Lodge** or **Curry Village Recreation Center** (209/372-1208 or 209/372-8323; 9am-6pm daily spring and fall, 8am-8pm daily summer)—or you can bring your own. With 12 miles (19.3 km) of smooth, paved bike paths, the **Yosemite Valley Bike Path** is one of the most popular rides in the park. Biking is also permitted on Yosemite's paved roads, but not on hiking trails. Children under 18 must wear helmets, and they are recommended for all bicyclists.

ROCK CLIMBING

With world-famous El Capitan and Half Dome, Yosemite is well known as a mecca for rock climbers. But even experienced climbers who have tackled high walls in parks and public lands near their homes are sometimes daunted when they get their first look at Yosemite Valley's massive vertical walls. If you don't have experience with granite crack climbing or traditional climbing, **Yosemite Mountaineering School and Guide Service** (209/372-8344; www.travelyosemite.com) offers rock-climbing classes in Yosemite Valley and near Tuolumne Meadows.

For those ready to climb on their own, **Supertopo Guides** (www.supertopo.com) is dedicated to a wealth of rock climbing "beta" (inside information) on Yosemite's big walls and the Tuolumne Meadows area (as well as other regions of the western United States). You'll find approach and descent facts, route histories, and lots of other details about the park's popular climbs.

DARK SKIES

Thanks to low humidity and a remote location far from urban glare, Yosemite lends itself to jet-black nights and clear skies—the perfect conditions for admiring the heavens. To see the Milky Way at its sparkly best, just lay out a blanket on any clear evening and enjoy the show. The higher the elevation, the better your view will be, which is why **Glacier Point, Tuolumne Meadows,** and **Tioga Pass** are popular stargazing spots. But to make sure your viewing won't be obstructed by car headlights or any other light pollution, you need to get away from roads and lighted buildings. So if you're really serious about seeing the stars, take a night hike (with a flashlight, of course). Great stargazing destinations include any of the easy-to-access domes, like **Sentinel Dome, Lembert Dome,** or **Pothole Dome.**

STARGAZING PROGRAMS

Starry Skies programs are held in Yosemite Valley and Glacier Point. **Starry Night Skies Over Yosemite** (888/413-8869; www.travelyosemite.com; 9pm daily summer, 8:30pm Sat.-Sun. winter; $10 per person) is offered every summer night in Yosemite Valley and on weekend nights in winter. During the one-hour walking tour, a naturalist explains the constellations visible over Yosemite Valley. Space is limited and reservations are required. **Glacier Point Starry Night Skies Over Yosemite** (888/413-8869; www.travelyosemite.com; Sun.-Thurs. June-Sept.; $67 adults, $46.50 ages 5-12) departs Yosemite Valley Lodge at 7pm on summer evenings, arriving at Glacier Point just before dark. Tours last about four hours and a one-hour astronomy program takes place after dark. If you can drive your own car to Glacier Point, you can pay $10 per person to participate in the one-hour stargazing program.

Stargazing programs are also held at **Tuolumne Meadows Campground** on clear nights at 9pm. Bring something to sit on, and dress warmly.

RAFTING

"River meandering" would be a better term for the river rafting on the **Merced River** in Yosemite Valley. Rafting is a matter of simply lying on your back, trailing a few fingers in the water, and gazing up at the granite walls as you float by. Sadly, the rafting season in Yosemite Valley is painfully short. The water level isn't usually low enough to be safe until late May or early June, and the season ends when the river gets too low and the rafts start scraping the river bottom, which is usually in late July.

During the months that the water level is safe, rafting and floating on the Merced River is allowed 10am-6pm daily. Life jackets are mandatory. Children under 50 pounds (23 kg) are not permitted on rafts. While you're out on the water, remember to protect the beautiful Merced River. If you choose to disembark, do so only on sandy beaches or gravel bars. Stay away from vegetated stream banks to protect the delicate riparian habitat.

You can rent an inflatable raft at **Curry Village Recreation Center** (209/372-8323; www.travelyosemite.com), or you can bring your own. You can also rent just life jackets, if you didn't bring one.

SWIMMING

With only a few exceptions, swimming is allowed in Yosemite's lakes and rivers. From mid-July to late September, plenty of swimming holes can be found along the **Merced River** on Yosemite Valley's east end. The sandy bars found here are ideal for lounging along the river and are also the most ecologically sound spots for entering and exiting the water. In the interest of protecting the Merced's fragile shoreline, always stay off grassy meadow areas. The easiest access to the river is at picnic areas such as Cathedral Beach or Sentinel Beach.

Avoid spring and early summer, when swimming anywhere in the Merced River is a very bad idea—the current can be much stronger than it looks. The same is true for the pools above Vernal and Nevada Falls, Illilouette Fall, and Upper Yosemite Fall. Although the water looks tempting after a hot and sweaty hike, even in late summer the current above these waterfalls can be deceptively swift—even deadly.

Swimming is **not allowed** in the Hetch Hetchy Reservoir (or within 1 mi/1.6 km upstream, such as at Rancheria Falls). Emerald Pool and Silver Apron, which are above Vernal Fall, and the Dana Fork of the Tuolumne River are also off limits to swimming.

WINTER SPORTS

Many seasoned Yosemite visitors insist that the best time to see the park is in winter. Crowds are nonexistent. **Snowshoeing** is as easy as walking, and no experience is required. Beginners can snowshoe amid the giant sequoia trees at the Merced Grove, Tuolumne Grove, or Mariposa Grove. More experienced snowshoers can head out from Badger Pass to Dewey Point, a 7-mile (11.3-km) round-trip, or follow one of several other marked snowshoe and cross-country ski trails from Badger Pass or Crane Flat. If you don't want to set out on your own, join a ranger-guided snowshoe walk. Snowshoe rentals are available at the **Mountain Shop in Curry Village** and **Badger Pass** on Glacier Point Road.

For skiing and snowboarding, Badger Pass is one of the mellowest ski resorts in the entire Sierra. Lift lines? High-priced lift tickets? No such thing here. If you don't feel like driving on snow-covered roads, you can take

floating on the Merced River

the shuttle bus to **Badger Pass** from Yosemite Valley Lodge. If you don't know how to ski or snowboard, Badger's 85 acres (34 ha) of slopes are the perfect place to learn. Lessons are offered daily. Or keep it simple—go "snow tubing" on the Badger Pass hills. It's just like sledding, only safer, because you are cushioned by a big billowy inner tube.

For more information, **Yosemite Winter Club** (http://yosemitewinterclub.com) is a website dedicated to promoting winter sports at Yosemite, including downhill skiing at Badger Pass, ice-skating in Yosemite Valley, and backcountry ski touring in Tuolumne Meadows.

RANGER PROGRAMS

Ranger programs take place throughout the park, except in the Hetch Hetchy area. Check the free Yosemite newspaper for a schedule of ranger walks, or inquire at a visitor center.

Ranger walks take place daily in Yosemite Valley and daily in the summer in the Wawona and Glacier Point area. Typical subjects include Yosemite's Indigenous people, bears, waterfalls, rock climbing, birds, and geology. Walks leave from various locations—the campgrounds, visitor centers, Happy Isles, and other Valley trailheads—throughout the day. Ranger walks are free; no reservations are necessary.

Specific ranger-led walks include 1.5-hour interpretive hikes through the lower grove of **Mariposa Grove of Giant Sequoias;** walks to the **Tuolumne Grove of Giant Sequoias;** hikes to **Taft Point, Sentinel Dome,** and **Illilouette Fall;** and walks to the top of **Lembert Dome** and **Pothole Dome** and along the **Tuolumne River.**

Ranger-led sit-down programs are held year-round at the **Lower Pines Campground Amphitheater** every summer morning and evening.

ACCESSIBILITY

People with permanent disabilities are entitled to an Access Pass, which provides free access to all federal fee areas, including all U.S. national parks and national forests. It also allows for discounted camping fees at some campgrounds. Access Passes are available at no cost from Yosemite visitor centers and entrance stations.

A free brochure on accessibility for wheelchair users and other physically challenged visitors is available by contacting the park, or by download from www.nps.gov/yose. **Wheelchair rentals** are available at the **Yosemite Medical Clinic** (9000 Ahwahnee Dr., Yosemite Valley; 209/372-4637) and at the **Yosemite Valley Lodge bike rental kiosk** (209/372-1208).

A **sign language interpreter** is available in the park in the summer months. To request in advance that the interpreter is available at a certain park event or activity, contact the rangers in any visitor center. All requests are filled on a first-come, first-served basis. Park orientation videos and slide shows in the Valley Welcome Center are captioned.

Tactile exhibits are found at the Valley Welcome Center and Happy Isles Art and Nature Center.

Cars with disabled-person placards are allowed access on the Happy Isles Loop and paved road to Mirror Lake, east of Curry Village. Disabled visitors who don't have a placard may obtain a temporary one from park visitor centers.

Spring through fall, travelers with disabilities who are unable to board the Mariposa Grove Tram may drive behind the tram and listen to an audio tour of the grove.

TRAVELING WITH CHILDREN

Yosemite and other national parks are ideal places to teach kids about nature and the environment. In Yosemite, kids can go for hikes, attend a campfire talk led by a park ranger, climb on rocks, help with camp chores, learn about animals that reside in the park, ride bikes, toast marshmallows, go rafting, ride horses, learn photography skills, or

just hang out in a meadow and be kids. The list of possible activities for children in Yosemite is endless—just as it is for adults.

The **Junior Ranger program,** popular at national parks across the country, is open to kids ages 7-13. Kids earn the official Junior Ranger badge by completing an activity book ($5), attending a one-hour Junior Ranger walk, and picking up a bag of litter to help keep the park clean. Junior Ranger walks are held daily during the summer. For more information, check the park's free newspaper, or ask in any visitor center. Younger kids (ages 3-6) can join in the Little Cubs program.

Wee Wild Ones is a free 45-minute interactive program for kids ages 6 and under, featuring stories, songs, games, crafts, and activities, mostly relating to the subject of Yosemite's animals. In the summer and fall, Wee Wild Ones occurs before evening programs held at the Yosemite Valley Lodge Amphitheater or the Curry Village Amphitheater. In winter and spring, this program is held during the day in front of the great fireplace in The Ahwahnee. Parents are encouraged to participate with their children.

TRAVELING WITH PETS

Traveling with your pet to any national park in the United States is a difficult proposition. Pets are not allowed in any lodging in Yosemite, and they are not allowed on the vast majority of trails. Pets are permitted in some campgrounds and in all parking lots and picnic areas. In campgrounds, they must be in your tent, RV, or car at night, or you risk having your pet tangle with a bear or other wild animal. Pets should never be left unattended. At all times, they must be physically restrained or attached to a leash 6 feet (1.8 m) long or shorter.

If you need to board your dog while you're in Yosemite, the closest location to Yosemite Valley is Yosemite **K9 Kennels in Foresta** (209/347-7983; www.

yosemitek9kennels.com). This privately run kennel has five outdoor stalls with shade for dogs. Dog owners must reserve online in advance and provide written proof of immunizations.

On top of all that, here's one more doggone rule to keep in mind: If you insist on bringing your dog to Yosemite, you are responsible for cleaning up after him or her, and you must put all "deposits" into the nearest trash receptacle.

The bottom line: Your dog will be happier somewhere else.

HEALTH AND SAFETY
EMERGENCY SERVICES
The **Yosemite Medical Clinic** (9000 Ahwahnee Dr., Yosemite Valley; 209/372-4637) can handle most emergencies big and small. In fact, they handle more than 10,000 of them every year. The clinic has experienced nursing staff, emergency physicians, a nurse practitioner, and support staff on duty. Emergency care is available 24 hours daily; drop-in visits and urgent care are available 8am-7pm daily. The nearest hospitals are in Sonora, Oakhurst, Merced, and Mammoth Lakes.

HAZARDS
Hiking
By far the biggest dangers to be faced in Yosemite are those created by visitors who don't follow posted rules and regulations. If a sign states "Stay Back from the Edge," obey it. Be wary of waterfalls, slick hiking trails, and cliffs and ledges with steep drop-offs. Remain on the trails to avoid getting lost or getting yourself into a hazardous situation. Always carry a good map. If you are heading out for a hike, tell someone where you are going and when you will be back. Carry a day pack with all the essentials for a day out and a few emergencies.

Drinking Water
Always carry water with you or be able to filter or purify water from natural sources like lakes, rivers, or streams.

The high-elevation air in the Sierra Nevada, combined with heat or wind, will dehydrate you much faster than you expect. Never, ever drink water from a natural source without purifying it. The microscopic organism *Giardia lamblia*, as well as other types of bacteria, may be found in backcountry water sources and can cause a litany of gastrointestinal problems. Only purifying, sterilizing, or boiling water from natural sources will eliminate these bad bugs.

A favorite purifier of many day hikers and backpackers is the **Steripen,** which sterilizes water using ultraviolet light. Dip your wide-mouthed water bottle into a lake or stream, then turn on your Steripen, immerse it in your bottle, and stir it around. In about 90 seconds, you have water that's safe to drink. Other options include bottle-style filters, which are almost as light as an empty plastic bottle and eliminate the need to carry both a filter and a bottle. Dip the bottle in the stream, screw on the top (which has a filter inside it), and squeeze the bottle to drink. The water is filtered on its way out of the squeeze top.

Altitude Sickness

Many hikers experience shortness of breath when hiking only a few thousand feet higher than the elevation at which they live. Some may notice slightly labored breathing while hiking at an elevation as low as 4,000 feet (1,220 m)—the exact elevation of Yosemite Valley. As you go higher, it may get worse, sometimes leading to headaches and nausea. It takes a full 72 hours to acclimate to major elevation changes, although most people feel better after a day or two.

The best preparation for hiking at high elevation is to sleep at that elevation, or as close to it as possible, the night before. If you are planning a strenuous hike at 7,000 feet (2,100 m) or above, spend a day or two beforehand taking easier hikes at the same elevation. Get plenty of rest, drink plenty of fluids, and avoid alcohol.

Serious altitude sickness typically occurs above 10,000 feet (3,000 m). It is generally preventable by simply allowing enough time for acclimation. Staying fully hydrated and fueled with food will also help. If you start to feel ill (nausea, vomiting, severe headache), you are experiencing altitude sickness. Some people can get by with taking aspirin and trudging onward, but if you are seriously ill, the only cure is to descend as soon as possible.

Lightning Strikes

If you see or hear a thunderstorm approaching, avoid exposed ridges and peaks. This may be disheartening advice when you're only 1 mile (1.6 km) from the summit of Clouds Rest, Half Dome, or Mount Hoffmann, but follow it anyway. If you're already on a mountaintop when a thunderstorm is threatening, stay out of enclosed places such as rock caves and recesses. Confined areas can be deadly in lightning storms. Do not lean against rock slopes or trees; try to keep a few feet of air space around you. Squat low on your boot soles, or sit on your day pack, jacket, or anything that will insulate you in case lightning strikes the ground.

Hantavirus

In August 2012, a rash of alarming media reports told of death and serious illness among Yosemite visitors, caused not by lightning, rockfall, or drowning, but by deer mice. The culprit was an infection known as hantavirus pulmonary syndrome (HPS), a rare but serious disease caused by a virus that can be contracted through contact with the urine, droppings, or saliva of deer mice. About 30 people in the United States come down with hantavirus annually. The disease has no known cure; about one-third of those who contract it will die.

Since the outbreak, the National Park Service and the park's concessionaires have gone to great lengths to reduce the possibility of mice entering the Curry Village cabins, which were linked to the 2012 outbreak. The 91

insulated signature tent cabins were demolished in December 2012. Only the single-walled tent cabins remain. No Curry Village hantavirus cases have been reported since the demolition.

The National Park Service urges visitors to avoid touching live or dead rodents or disturbing rodent burrows, dens, or nests. They also recommend that visitors keep food in tightly sealed containers, including those stored in bear boxes, so rodents can't get to it. Overnight visitors should contact housekeeping or maintenance if they see rodents or rodent signs, including droppings or urine, in their lodgings.

RESOURCES

Yosemite National Park
www.nps.gov/yose
This official National Park Service website for Yosemite provides up-to-date information on current road and weather conditions, lodging and camping options, park rules and regulations, and wilderness permits. (The same information can be obtained by phone at 209/372-0200.) A printable travel guide is available, and you may request maps and information about Yosemite to be mailed to your home. In addition to plentiful visitor data, the website also has online exhibits on Yosemite's natural history, human history, and geology, as well as information on jobs in Yosemite, current management plans for the park, and a wide range of related links.

Yosemite National Park YouTube Channel
www.youtube.com/user/yosemite-nationalpark
Yosemite National Park posts all of its official videos here, including its Yosemite Nature Notes video podcast series. Topics include general visitor information like how to get to the park, where to hike, and where to find overnight lodging as well as the natural history of frogs, bears, and beavers.

Yosemite Conservancy
www.yosemite.org
The Yosemite Conservancy was formed in 2010 to merge the Yosemite Association and the Yosemite Fund, two nonprofits dedicated to supporting the park through visitor services, sales of books and maps, and membership activities, as well as granting funds for managing wildlife, restoring habitat, creating educational exhibits, and repairing trails in the park. The Yosemite Conservancy operates visitor center bookstores throughout the park and offers a wide range of educational courses through Yosemite Outdoor Adventures. Its website provides information on a range of educational park activities that include art classes in Yosemite Valley, performances at the Yosemite Theater, and backpacking trips to the Lyell Glacier. It also includes information on how to become a conservancy member, how to contribute to various work projects in the park, current Yosemite weather conditions, upcoming seminars and events, news stories, and a webcam with live shots of Yosemite Valley.

Yosemite Hikes
www.yosemitehikes.com
This website is a veritable encyclopedia of all things Yosemite. Day hiking information is the main focus, but this clever and comprehensive site also includes tour itineraries, lodging and wildflower information, and photo galleries. The hundreds of images on this site are nothing short of awesome.

Reservations
Aramark's Yosemite Hospitality
www.travelyosemite.com
The park concessionaire, Yosemite Hospitality, a subsidiary of Aramark, handles all of Yosemite's in-park accommodations, tours, events, and organized activities, all of which are described on this site. You can get information and make reservations at this website (or by

phone at 888/413-8869). Whether you want to stay at a hotel in Yosemite Valley, buy a ski pass, or sign up for a guided tour, everything you need is found here.

Camping and Half Dome Permits
National Recreation Reservation Service
www.recreation.gov

Visitors seeking to camp in or near Yosemite can make campground reservations at this site or by phoning 877/444-6777 or 518/885-3639 from outside the United States and Canada. Reservations are available up to five months in advance at one of three reservable campgrounds in Yosemite Valley or one of four reservable campgrounds elsewhere in the park. Reservations are also available at many national forest campgrounds a few miles outside the park borders, particularly in the Sierra National Forest. This website also handles all reservations for Half Dome day hiking permits.

INDEX

LIST OF MAPS

PHOTO CREDITS

Get inspired for your next adventure

Follow **@moonguides** on Instagram or subscribe to our newsletter at **moon.com**

#TravelWithMoon

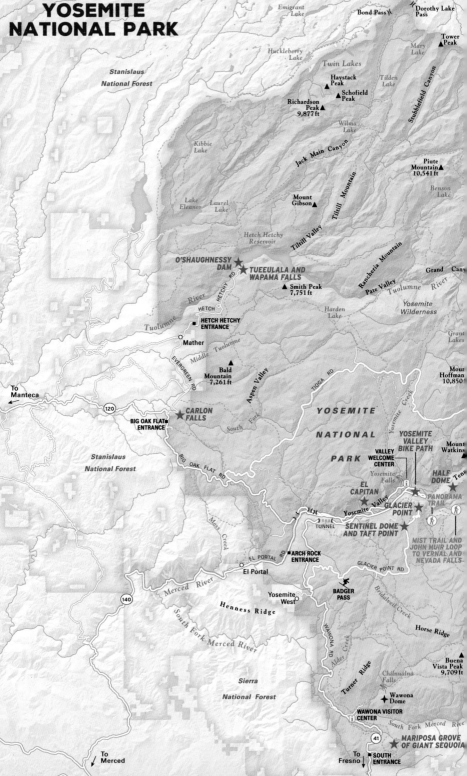

MOON

- BEST OF -
YOSEMITE

Ann Marie Brown